Ruth Hubbard and Gilles Paquet

Irregular Governance

A Plea for Bold Organizational Experimentation

| Collaborative Decentred Metagovernance Series

This series of books is designed to define cumulatively the contours of collaborative decentred metagovernance. At this time, there is still no canonical version of this paradigm: it is *en émergence*. This series intends to be one of many 'construction sites' to experiment with various dimensions of an effective and practical version of this new approach.

Metagovernance is the art of combining different forms or styles of governance, experimented with in the private, public and social sectors, to ensure effective coordination when power, resources and information are widely distributed, and the governing is of necessity decentred and collaborative.

The series invites conceptual and practical contributions focused on different issue domains, policy fields, *causes célèbres*, functional processes, etc. to the extent that they contribute to sharpening the new apparatus associated with collaborative decentred metagovernance.

In the last few decades, there has been a need felt for a more sophisticated understanding of the governing of the private, public and social sectors: for less compartmentalization among sectors that have much in common; and for new conceptual tools to suggest new relevant questions and new ways to carry out the business of governing, by creatively recombining the tools of governance that have proven successful in all these sectors. These efforts have generated experiments that have been sufficiently rich and wide-ranging in the various laboratories to warrant efforts to pull together what we know at this stage.

The eighth book in the series is an irreverent challenge to administrative conservatorship, and a case for bold organizational experimentation. It makes the case for effective new actors, new structural forms and new social technologies, while showing the perils of ill-conceived contraptions like super-bureaucracies, single-purpose agencies and failure to pay due attention to good management.

Interested parties are invited to join the Chautauqua.

– Editorial Board

Other titles published by INVENIRE are listed at the end of this book.

Ruth Hubbard and Gilles Paquet

Irregular Governance

A Plea for Bold Organizational Experimentation

INVENIRE

Ottawa, Canada
2015

University of Ottawa **Press**
Les **Presses** de l'Université d'Ottawa

The University of Ottawa Press (UOP) is proud to be the oldest of the francophone university presses in Canada and the oldest bilingual university publisher in North America. Since 1936, UOP has been enriching intellectual and cultural discourse by producing peer-reviewed and award-winning books in the humanities and social sciences, in French and in English.

www.Press.uOttawa.ca

Library and Archives Canada Cataloguing in Publication

Title: Irregular governance : a plea for bold organizational experimentation / Ruth Hubbard and Gilles Paquet.

Names: Container of (work): Paquet, Gilles. Ombuds as producers of governance. | Container of (work): Hubbard, Ruth, 1942- P3 and the 'porcupine' problem.

Series: Collaborative decentred metagovernance series ; v. 8.

Description: Series statement: Collaborative decentred metagovernance series ; 8 | Reprint. Originally published: Ottawa, Canada : Invenire, 2015. | Includes bibliographical references.

Identifiers: Canadiana (print) 20220285292 | Canadiana (ebook) 20220285314 | ISBN 9780776638430 (softcover) | ISBN 9780776638447 (PDF) | ISBN 9780776638454 (EPUB)

Subjects: LCSH: Public administration. | LCSH: Organizational effectiveness. | LCSH: Administrative agencies.

Classification: LCC JF1351 .I77 2022 | DDC 351—dc23

Legal Deposit: Library and Archives Canada, Third Quarter 2022
© University of Ottawa Press 2022, all rights reserved.

This book was initially published by Invenire Books in 2015 in the Collaborative Decentered Metagovernance Series. The cover design, layout and design were produced by Sandy Lynch. The University of Ottawa Press reissued this book thanks to the support of Ontario Creates.

Invenire

Invenire Books, an Ottawa-based idea factory that operated from 2010 to 2019, specialized in collaborative governance and stewardship. Invenire and its authors provide creative practical and stimulating responses to the challenges and opportunities faced by today's organizations. The list is now carried by the University of Ottawa Press.

The University of Ottawa Press gratefully acknowledges the support extended to its publishing list by the Government of Canada, the Canada Council for the Arts, the Ontario Arts Council, the Social Sciences and Humanities Research Council and the Canadian Federation for the Humanities and Social Sciences through the Awards to Scholarly Publications Program, and by the University of Ottawa.

ONTARIO ARTS COUNCIL
CONSEIL DES ARTS DE L'ONTARIO
an Ontario government agency
un organisme du gouvernement de l'Ontario

Canada Council   Conseil des arts
for the Arts   du Canada

Canadä

uOttawa

| Table of Contents

INTRODUCTION

| Beyond Conservatorship

*"... le travail de l'ironiste ... rendre historique,
donc conjoncturel, donc contingent, ce que le sens
commun juge nécessaire et fondamental ..."*
Chantal Delsol

There is a particular tradition in public administration
defending the view that the primary function of the
bureaucracy is to protect, maintain and preserve the
administrative institutions in a manner consistent with
constitutional processes, traditions, values and beliefs (Friedrich
1963). For those holding this view, the notion of *administrative
conservatorship* shapes the manner in which the role of career
executives is defined: "balancing the inherent tension in the
political system between the need to *serve* and the need to
preserve" (Terry 2003: 29).

Such a conservatory bias may seem to be innocuous, but
it can be rather toxic. Over time, the bureaucracy's need to
preserve appeared to have overshadowed its duty to serve.
This movement may not be dominant in the schools of public
administration around the world, but it has had an important
impact on the pan-Canadian scene where the tradition of an
independent professional public service has been revered. A
fair number of opinion-moulders have seized this movement
as providing opportune legitimization for the imperium of

tradition, and some version of its gospel has been propounded (Heintzman 2014).

This worldview has fed an unhealthy tendency to sacralize the role of the bureaucracy as guardian of the fundamental principles of democracy, and to allow the bureaucratic clergy to define what has to be preserved; and this sort of hijacking has been anointed by a plurality of public administration academics (Aucoin 2012).

However, since the bureaucracy is not a selfless clergy – whatever those who regard bureaucrats as missionaries may say (Kernaghan 2007) – this movement has guided the bureaucracy's strategy in defining what needed to be preserved: preserving most things that helped the bureaucracy maintain its own power base and putative dominium.

This imperative duty to preserve has often served as a rationale:

- for public administrators to act in ways that pose a threat to the public good, generate disloyalty to elected officials (even when the latter's guidance stays within the confines of the constitution and the law), and open the door to elevating the welfare of the bureaucratic tribe to the level of first priority behind a cloak of conservatorship ideals; and,

- for public administrators and their academic supporters to adopt the *administrative conservatorship attitude/dogma* as a legitimate port of entry to the pursuit of purposes other than the common good (Terry 2003: chapter 6). For those holding a degree of suspicion about this sort of state clergy, such a rogue pursuit is not a possibility but a probability (Paquet 2014: chapter 4), and it is likely not only to generate abuses but also to serve as a toxic rationale for combating change and innovation.

Conservatorship as a mental prison

One major bias of administrative conservators is to presume that most organizations and associations are purposive arrangements in which members are engaged in joint enterprises seeking the satisfaction of some common substantive wants (Oakeshott 1975: 205). Within such *purposive associations* (be they businesses, unions, churches, states, etc.), the guidance system is a matter of management. There is a propensity to believe that it can only be run top-down, hierarchically – focused on well-defined collective purposes on which there is a consensus. Unsurprisingly, reference to 'leadership' ensues.

Civil associations are quite different. They have no substantive ends as such, and each individual or group action is the result of individuals or groups pursuing their own particular objectives – with various conflicts and collisions being resolved by means of agreed-upon rules or conventions (Spicer 2001: 22).

In earlier writings (Paquet 2011: chapter 2), it has been suggested that over the recent decades, as the context has become more complex and turbulent, and as power, resources and information have come to be more widely distributed into many hands, there has been a dramatic shift in all sectors from purposive arrangements to ones that are closer to civil organizations, from Big G (Government) top-down governing to small-g (governance) more participative and collaborative governing. This shift has meant that the whole organizational order has come to be characterized less and less by a commonality of values, and less and less by claims that anyone is fully in charge. Stewardship – an assortment of mechanisms ensuring the requisite guidance (as in the case of automatic pilots in aircrafts) – has come to be regarded as the notion that 'best fits' (i.e., what is required) to ensure effective coordination in these circumstances (Hubbard *et al.* 2012).

This shift has triggered a variety of consequences.

First, administrative conservators have tended to remain trapped in the Big G world – the world of common values and common purposes – at a time when diversity of values and variety of purposes have become the norm. This has led them to give relatively less attention to the governance challenges looming large in the world of civic associations: such as finding ways to synoptically blend the representations of the many groups in order to elicit tractable, acceptable and promising directions for the association; and finding ways to design an array of incentives, conventions and moral contracts likely to provide the requisite motivations and capacities for members to collaborate effectively.

Second, short-term concerns, built on convenient, somewhat surreal, and unduly stylized representations of the world, have come to dominate the scene, with a focus on maintaining and preserving the *status quo ante* – another word for resilience in the most circumscribed sense of the term (Paquet 2005: chapter 5).

On both fronts, administrative conservatorship has led to exercises in the distortion of concepts like leadership and resilience to give them a contrived form necessary to ensure that they remain somewhat useable in new circumstances (e.g., collective leadership, leaderless leadership, etc.) rather than to experiments with new approaches to face head-on and effectively the stewardship challenges posed by the new environments.

This indulgence at the conceptual level could only lead to a muddling-though at the analytical level. To a considerable extent, conservatorship has contributed to embalming new critical issues in familiar conservatory terms, instead of recognizing the need to adapt the conceptual and governing apparatus to take into account the new dimensions of interest exposed by the emergence of the new challenges. The conservatorship attitude has prompted a regular approach to public administration that could only be characterized as fundamentally dysfunctional.

Irregular governance as a response to emergent environments

Irregular governance pertains to the exploration and design of unusual or, at least, less habitual forms of governance, in order to deal more effectively with emerging forms of turbulence and complexity in the environment and the consequent texture of the social order. These new circumstances constitute both challenges and opportunities to develop new prototypes and designs that might be better able to cope with the new circumstances. But they do not only open the door for such new initiatives, they also often create conditions that enable conservatory forces to reinforce their dominium by encouraging the maintenance of old conservatory arrangements and practices. These contraptions may be perilous for our democratic order.

So, whatever the dangers of exploration with new prototypes – for they may prove inadequate – on balance, it would appear preferable to mindlessly embrace the old conceptual frameworks and antiquated organizational forms that have proven to be grossly ineffective, or to allow refurbished versions of such contraptions to become installed.

Our intention here is not to survey the broad field of all the old and new defective conceptual frameworks and organizational forms, and suggest improved substitutes across the board. More modestly, we report on both some innovative initiatives and some perilous situations that have appeared to us as relatively consequential at three levels: emergence of new actors, new structures and new technologies.

On the innovative initiative front, we focus on an example of a new actor, new structure and new technology (either implemented, or which should be implemented), that would appear to be helpful in improving the requisite inquiring system, and the requisite stewardship for progressivity and antifragility.[1] On the perilous situations front, we focus on an example of a toxic new actor, new structure and of inadequate technology generating poor productivity and progressivity

[1] On these somewhat heretical notions, some forewarning may be useful. On the notions of inquiring systems and stewardship, see Paquet and Wilson (2011). Progressivity connotes **not** the popular notion of progressiveness (which has an income- and wealth-redistributive and social-democratic flavour, and is in good currency in social-democratic circles), but the notion of the capacity to transform that is likely to allow innovation to spread at optimal speed – a notion developed by François Perroux (1960) that has been used widely in more recent times (Paquet 2013). Similarly, the notion of antifragility does **not** connote the notion of resilience as springing back to the *status quo ante* after a shock, but rather the more ambitious aim to ensure that arrangements, organizations and social systems get stronger, and more robust and innovative, as a result of increased disorder and shocks in a turbulent environment (Taleb 2012).

in the public household on the Canadian scene, and entailing much fragility for the social order.

Initiatives and perils are many at the three levels. We can only hope that the cases we have used to illustrate the positive and the negative at each level will convey as well as possible the possibilities open to the social designer interested in refurbishing the personnel, the structure and the technology of organizations and institutions, but also the potential dangers that might materialize as a result of some perverse and toxic reactions to the pressures from the new turbulent internal and external environments.

The rest of the volume proceeds in three stages.

First, as complexity and turbulence in the environment increase, the collaborative governance protocols function more or less satisfactorily, and reveal gaps in the texture of the organizational and institutional fabric. Some roles and functions, not perceived as useful in the past, come to the attention of the stakeholders as organizational failures materialize. New actors appear to be needed in this emergent world, and the new interest in 'ombudsmanship' has been a response to such felt need.

However, such pressures need not necessarily generate entirely new actors or prototypes. Often, the internal dynamics of self-defence of existing actors may lead to some of them seizing the opportunity that opens itself to aggrandize their influence, and fill the vacuum. The existing bureaucracies have been quite opportunistic in taking advantage of the new challenges to reinforce their position – the more aggressively so when the administrative conservatorship philosophy would appear to provide a rationale for doing so. We have examined the emergence of a problematic new group of super-bureaucrats in the recent past as an epiphenomenon of the new culture of adjudication that has followed the large number of mishaps that have occurred in our higher risk and more complex world.

Secondly, we have probed other gaps that have not generated new actors, but have fostered new organizational forms. While standard private, public and civic models of organizations have proved effective in dealing with many of the tasks and challenges faced by the public sector, more recently it has become obvious that mixed forms of organizations (mixing features from the standard public, private and social sectors) might provide better and cheaper delivery of public goods to citizens. We have used the growth of the public-private partnerships as a case in point.

Yet, the reflex to 'complexify' the design of organizations in order to incorporate a broader range of instruments/ motivations has not always been dominant. In the face of more complex and wicked problems, administrative conservatorship has often prompted a return to narrow and highly-focused organizational forms in the name of the bow-arrow-target mentality of yesteryear. In a world requiring broader synoptic perspectives (Brown et al. 2010; Paquet 2014: conclusion), this sort of reaction has often generated disastrous situations. We have illustrated this sort of toxicity by looking at some single purpose entities.

Thirdly, we have also drawn attention to other pressures – too often ignored and resisted because they were simply calling for new ways of doing things. These are cases where new social technologies might be in order, but where the conservatorship mentality is likely to occlude the problem and to deny the need for change and innovation. We have examined these challenges in two steps.

In the first instance, we probe the process of innovation as redesign. We have stylized the carousel of innovation, shown what operations it entails, and illustrated how innovation has succeeded in overcoming the challenges in two issue domains: retooling on the fiscal front in the restaurant business, and restructuring in the forestry sector.

In the second instance, we have noted the various ways in which observers have underlined the toxicity of the weaknesses of the management process in the public sector (as a source of lack both of productivity and progressivity denounced by numerous reports to the Clerk of Privy Council over the years), and suggested two complementary ways in which the management vacuum, responsible for much of the underperformance of the public household, might be repaired, but have been successfully resisted:

- putting in place an enabling board of management structure to ensure that broad policy goals are pursued in a managerially competent way; and,
- developing a meaningful management technology to match job requirement capabilities and individual competencies, to refurbish the extraordinarily unproductive human resource management in good currency, especially at the senior levels in the public service.

Those gaps in the texture of public administration are not the only ones, and the fact that the public administration enterprise is so blind to so many fundamental gaps and misfits in the architecture, engineering and *meccano* of public administration may not be ascribable exclusively to the philosophy of administrative conservatorship, but conservatorship has played an important role in it.

In conclusion, we make a case for three avenues to kick start the required process of organizational/institutional refurbishment: focus on eunomics and broad ways to approach the governance challenges; recognize the need for irreverence in order to neutralize the conservatorship philosophy; and adopt much more ambitious guideposts in the design of the inquiry underpinning the process of social learning at the core of stewardship – not being satisfied with seeking stability and resilience, but explicitly seeking progressivity and antifragility.

Acknowledgements and disclaimer

This short book deals with big problems, and suggests that they can only be tackled by unorthodox means. Sticking to the usual methods and practicing conservatorship is most certainly not promising. Gambling on irregular governance is no panacea, but it is immensely more promising.

Arguing for more critical thinking, more irreverence, and even some cruelty in dealing with existing arrangements runs counter to the basic ethos of preserving. But it may be time for boldness, and time to recognize that more importance needs to be given to innovation if progress toward a more eunomic social order is what is truly sought.

As always, we are most grateful for the many-faceted support for our work by the Centre on Governance of the University of Ottawa, but, in the case of this particular book, we feel the need to add that the Centre should **not** be held responsible for either our irreverent questioning of the existing social order (or for our forceful language at times in so doing). The editorial assistance of Anne Burgess is gratefully acknowledged.

References

Aucoin, Peter. 2012. "New Political Governance in Westminster Systems: Impartial Public Administration and Management Performance at Risk," *Governance: An international journal of policy, administration and institutions*, 25(2): 177-199.

Brown, Valerie A., John A. Harris and Jacqueline Y. Russell (eds.). 2010. *Tackling Wicked Problems: Through the Transdisciplinary Imagination*. London, UK: Earthscan.

Friedrich, Carl J. 1963. *Man and His Government*. New York, NY: McGraw-Hill.

Heintzman, Ralph. 2014. *Renewal of the Federal Public Service: Toward a Charter of Public Service*. Ottawa, ON: Canada 2020 (www.canada2020.ca).

Hubbard, Ruth *et al.* 2012. *Stewardship: Collaborative Decentred Metagovernance and Inquiring Systems*. Ottawa, ON: Invenire Books.

Kernaghan, Kenneth. 2007. *A Special Calling: Values, Ethics, and Professional Public Service*. Ottawa, ON: Canada Public Service Agency.

Oakeshott, Michael. 1975. *On Human Conduct*. Oxford, UK: Oxford University Press.

Paquet, Gilles. 2005. *Gouvernance : une invitation à la subversion*. Montreal, QC: Liber.

Paquet, Gilles. 2011. *Gouvernance collaborative : un antimanuel*. Montreal, QC: Liber.

Paquet, Gilles. 2013. *Tackling Wicked Policy Problems: Equality, Diversity and Sustainability*. Ottawa, ON: Invenire Books.

Paquet, Gilles. 2014. *Unusual Suspects: Essays on Social Learning Disabilities*. Ottawa, ON: Invenire Books.

Paquet, Gilles and Christopher Wilson. 2011. "Collaborative Co-governance as Inquiring Systems," *www.optimumonline.ca*, 41(2): 1-12.

Perroux, François. 1960. *L'univers économique et social*. Tome IX de l'Encyclopédie française. Paris, FR: Larousse.

Spicer, Michael W. 2001. *Public Administration and the State – A Postmodern Perspective*. Tuscaloosa, AL: University of Alabama Press.

Taleb, Nassim N. 2012. *Antifragile – Things that gain from disorder*. New York, NY: Random House.

Terry, Larry D. 2003. *Leadership of Public Bureaucracies – The Administrator as Conservator*. Armonk, NY: M.E. Sharpe.

PART I
New Mediating Actors

CHAPTER 1

| Ombuds as Producers of Governance: Initiative I

Gilles Paquet

"Je laisse à d'autres le soin d'inquiéter,
de terroriser et de continuer de tout confondre."
René Magritte

Preamble

This is a think piece. It is not meant to provide a definitive answer to the question of how justice will be ensured, how the role of 'ombuds' and other less formal agents should evolve, and how 'ombudsing' and other forms of less formal despatches of justice might differ from place to place. On such matters, practitioners should have the final say. This chapter aims only to provoke some reflection on these questions, with a view to breaking out of the box of conventional thinking.

The chapter deals with two separate problems: first, the need to broaden the concept of justice; second, the expanding of the role of ombuds in this new territory.

The first part is an examination of the problem of access to justice in a world that is becoming more diverse, complex and turbulent. It has been argued explicitly in the last decade that the formal justice system may not be serving the community well, and that a more distributed, multiple-access, and open-source system of justice should be put in place.

The second part argues for a more creative role for ombuds, and seeks to enlarge the portfolio of governance mechanisms by factoring in ombuds as producers of governance, and particularly important agents of the governance of justice through their mediation work.

The judgment of wider courts

The expression "wider courts" may not be elegant, but it serves to draw attention to the fact that the notion of access to justice does not only mean access to the courts and to the formal legal apparatus. The problem was raised in the year 2000 in a symposium organized by Justice Canada on the theme of *Expanding Horizons: Rethinking Access to Justice in Canada*. It was an invitation by the legal establishment to use lateral thinking in developing strategies for better ways to provide access to justice for Canadians.

At that 2000 meeting, many experts acknowledged the acute nature of the problem: a message of anxiety on the part of Justice Turpel-Lafond with regard to the way the justice system treats Aboriginal groups; a message of disconnection between the formal system of lawyers and courts and the real living law of everyday interaction from the former head of the Law Reform Commission of Canada, Roderick Macdonald; and a plea for more opportunities for citizens to participate more fully in the lawmaking process. There was also a message of denunciation by the philosopher Jacques Dufresne, who claimed that the formal judicial institution – *the fortress* – is preventing the normal carrying out of justice, and is actually a source of injustice because of the lack of preventive justice. He argued for a *justice douce* (Paquet 2000).

Whether what is needed is more prevention, better connection, or more restorative justice, or something else, it was noted that there were already alternative processes providing justice outside the formal system, and there was a need for more of it, and of a more ambitious sort.

New mechanisms for a paradoxical world

The search for new mechanisms for access to justice has emerged from the diversity of contexts, principles, and circumstances. But if one-size-fits-all appears to be unsatisfactory, then there is perhaps a need (in the name of fairness) for agreement on some *basic principles* – a sort of Magna Carta. This would guide the exploration of the new initiatives, and would focus on *'local justice'* – an effort to work at the level of the different groups, disputes, issues, etc. where it might be possible to fine-tune better practices – rather than through broad-ranging accords (Elster 1992).

Finding workable arrangements may not be easy in our paradoxical world.

Two paradoxes need to be resolved: (1) the one pitching local justice against substantive equality; and (2) the one pitching inclusion and participation in the justice process against representative democracy.

Equal but different would appear to be the foundation of the new flexible system, based on local justice and on the acceptance that there might be various windows to give access to justice. To resolve this paradox, an agreement on principles at the meta-level is needed: general principles defining the corridor of acceptable differences and permissible variety. The challenge is for jurists to generate such foundational meta-solutions.

The inclusion of the citizen more directly (upstream through alternative avenues to the formal legal process, or downstream in the case of restorative law) would indeed challenge the democratic method of choosing officials and allowing them to take decisions for the collectivity. These new ways short-circuit what is regarded as due process. This will require a major re-interpretation of the very notion of representative democracy: this constitutes yet another significant challenge for jurists.

In the short run, what is required is a guide to the necessary exploration: defining what is the corridor of permissible variations within the corridor of justice. What is also required is much more experimentation and a better knowledge of what succeeded and failed.

In the longer run, what one might first hope for is *a refurbishment of our philosophy of justice*, one that might be rooted in what Amartya Sen (1999) has put at the centre of the whole process of social, economic and political development – the freedom from different servitudes, or the elimination of 'unfreedoms' due to the lack of political margins of maneuverability, of social opportunities, of economic possibilities, and of transparency and security guarantees. Second, it is necessary to strive for the establishment of a *distributed and open-source justice system* – a system where justice is available in a variety of forms, from a variety of sources, and through a variety of channels, so as to ensure that the citizen has true access to justice.

But this cannot be tackled at a general level. Too many local forces of dynamic conservatism are at work to maintain the *status quo*. The problem must be tackled piecemeal by developing segmented experiments with already existing tools or instruments that are promising but have been underused and are under-developed. This is the road of least resistance: experiments in many loci using different ways of widening the 'existing courts' not only to open new trails but to establish new ways of producing governance. Among the most promising of these is to experiment with the burden of office of ombudspersons as producers of governance.

Ombuds as producers of governance

Fifty years ago, the very word ombudsman, and the institution attached to it, meant nothing to most people outside of Scandinavia. Now it is common currency in some one hundred countries. The main reason for this phenomenal growth has been the emergence of big government, and the consequent need for someone to protect the citizen from unfair decisions by Big G government. The same rationale holds for the private and social sectors, whose potentates have also required a watchdog. Ombudsing activities have contributed significantly to remedying the damage caused by the abusive powers of agents of these diverse potentates.

But in recent times, the context has changed: decentralized organizations have become the new world of work, so governing systems have become more complex, and the problems of coordination more 'wicked.' Most issues faced by citizens today are the results of a multiplicity of interwoven multi-sectoral forces, agents, groups and organizations, more or less consciously shaping the context in concert (Gregory and Giddings 2000). We have moved in all sectors from Big G government to small g governance – from a world of command-and-control to a world of coordinate-and-cultivate (Paquet 1999, 2005a; Malone 2004).

The role of ombudspersons has changed in this new world. It is a world where no one is completely in charge; where abuse emerges not from a single source, but from a constellation of actors from all sectors, who each have a piece of the information, of the power, and of the resources; where the source of abuse is diffuse, polycentric and systemic; where consensus is often unattainable; where conflict resolution can only be arrived at by creative compromise, negotiation, and organizational redesign; where issues need clarification, bargaining needs to be more effective, and new arrangements need to be experimented and played with; and all this when the modern democratic ethos seems to encourage political correctness and failure to confront (and therefore to discourage creative conflict), i.e., at a time when creative conflict resolution is becoming crucially important in our bargaining society (Johansen 1979).

In this new context where there are multiple principals and multiple rights holders (Grandori 2004), it is no longer sufficient for the ombuds to act as a shield: to assuage individual mistreatments, and to try to poke at elusive scapegoats. The ombuds must also, and more importantly, work to attenuate the malefits of what can only be called the *systemic governance failures* caused by multiple forces through dealing explicitly with their systemic sources. This does not reduce the importance of protecting widows and orphans, and of ensuring that individual wounds are taken care of, but it underlines that the ombuds' burden of office goes beyond these duties. What is required is the capacity to detect governance flaws at the origin of these mishaps, and to help launch the process that will ensure that the governance apparatus is appropriately repaired. The trigger may still be personal damage and complaints, but the answer can no longer be only personal reparation. It must also entail eliciting what might be a plausible and reasonable appreciation of the nature of the dysfunction, and some promising organizational redesign and architectural repairs to the governance apparatus.

The independence, accessibility, informality, low cost, and speed of the ombudsing process, together with the powers of investigation (*inquiry* may be a better word), and some form of statutory base of operation – all these features make ombudsing better suited to appreciate the new fluid realities, and better prepared to deal with governance failures than the more traditional legal (more rigid) and political (less reliable) processes. This explains why the ombudsing process would appear to be the instrument of choice in the small g governance world.

But all institutions are mortgaged to their past. Righting the wrongs done to citizens by public authorities (or by other potentates) by obtaining reparation, case by case, through meek interventions, has long been the main focus of ombuds' activities. This may explain why, in general, the ombuds have often been slow in recognizing the shift from Big G to small g, and therefore have failed, in many cases, to acknowledge the important new challenges facing them, and have not taken the necessary steps to transform the nature of their capabilities and practice so as to prepare them to perform such a task well.

In the rest of this chapter, we first sketch the features of the new environment faced by ombuds, underline the new importance of the pathologies of governance at the root of the mishaps they observe daily, surmise that there have been costs attached to the reluctance to delve into these pathologies as forcefully as one might like, and reflect on the inefficiency of the ombuds process as a result of it. Second, this state of affairs suggests that some effort at reinventing the ombuds' burden of office is in order, so we suggest what needs to be done – and in what manner – to make bargaining less inefficient, rationality more ecological, and experimentation more likely to be undertaken and to succeed. Some guideposts for this voyald are provided.

From Big G to small g: a tectonic change

We live in an era when the ground is in motion, and on-going interacting economic, financial, technological, social, political and legal change are the key drivers. Turbulence is the outcome of this mix of interacting transformational forces. Rosenau has proposed a label to convey the basic nature of this new epoch – *fragmegration*. It draws attention to the joint dynamics of centralization and decentralization, of localizing and globalizing, and of fragmentation and integration that are unleashed in this new world (Rosenau 2003).

'Fragmegration'

This is an era of organization-breaking, of weak and failed states, of distributed stewardship: the nation-state and other potentates are losing their dominance. This does not mean that nations disappear or states vanish; the state is less prominent, and is called upon to play some new, different, and somewhat attenuated roles. Organizational refurbishing is therefore most important (Fukuyama 2004). The institutional tsunami in progress has not yet, however, fully revealed its emergent outcome – the shape of the new type of public sector *en émergence*, for instance.

One thing is sure, however: the boundaries between the private, public and social (civic) spheres – never well-defined either conceptually or statistically in the former era – do not correspond to a rigid frontier. In the world of governance, they are becoming a wavering and evolving zone of fracture between subsets of organizations and institutions that are characterized by different integrating mechanisms (Paquet 1996-97). Power, resources and information are being distributed increasingly widely throughout the terrain of private, public and civic organizations. One of the main challenges for societal governance is to engineer the requisite coordination through *networked ecologies of governance* (Paquet 1995).

This new fluid institutional reality is made up of three generic ensembles of organizations, dominated by different integrating mechanisms – *quid pro quo exchange* (market economy), *coercion* (polity), and *gift or solidarity or reciprocity* (community and society). Kenneth Boulding (1970) used a simple triangle as a mapping device – with each of these families of integrating mechanisms in its purest form at one of the apexes, and all the inner territory representing organizations and institutions embodying different mixes of these integrative mechanisms.

There has been a tendency for the new socio-economy to trigger the development of an ever larger number of *mixed* institutions, blending these different mechanisms to some extent (e.g., market-based public regulation, public-private-social partnering, corporate social responsibility, etc.) in order to provide the necessary signposts and orientation maps in a new, confused and confusing world. This has translated into a much denser filling in of the Boulding triangle: mixed institutions capable of providing the basis for mediation, cooperation, harmonization, *concertation*, and even co-decisions involving agents or organizations from the three sectors (Laurent and Paquet 1998).

One can stylize this development via a series of emerging concentric circles within which there are different degrees of *institutional and organizational métissage* (Hubbard and Paquet 2002). This is depicted in Figure 1.

FIGURE 1. The Adapted Boulding Triangle

Economy

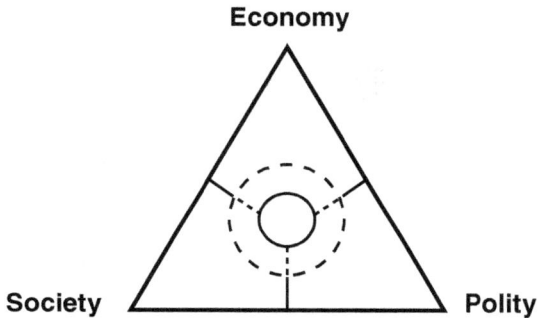

Society   **Polity**

Source: Kenneth E. Boulding. 1970. *A Primer on Social Dynamics*. New York, NY: The Free Press.

At any one time, a more or less integrated governance pattern brings people, architecture, routines, and cultures into an arrangement that generates good performance. Such a coherent pattern is rarely unique and permanent as circumstances evolve. Two centrally important minimal characteristics of this process of co-evolution (of the system and its environment) and joint evolution (economy, society, polity) are

- *resilience* (the capacity for the economy-polity-society nexus to spring back undamaged from the pressure or shock emerging from the environment, through some slight rearrangements that do not modify the nature of the overall system);[1] and,
- *learning* (the capacity to improve current performance, as a result of experience, through a redefinition of the overall objectives; and a modification of behaviour and structures as a result of new circumstances) (Schön 1971).

These characteristics are in creative tension, since resilience calls for preservation, while learning means change. Ideally, they must be kept in balance, yet with a tilt towards innovation.

---

[1] A less minimal requirement might be antifragility: the capacity not only to spring back undamaged from shocks from the environment, but to spring back stronger and more innovative from such ordeals (Taleb 2012).

Managing this tension well demands a capacity to switch to a greater or lesser dependence on one family of integrative mechanisms or another as circumstances change. To cope with an environment that is turbulent and generates surprises, organizations and societies must use their environment strategically in much the same way as the surfer uses the wave to adapt more quickly.

This calls for non-centralization for two reasons.

First, because the game of learning is going to generate more innovation if the component parts of a system, when confronted with local challenges, are empowered to take decisions on the spot (Naisbitt 1994). In fact, the best learning experience in this kind of world can be carried out through highly decentralized and flexible teams, woven by moral contracts and reciprocal obligations, negotiated in the context of evolving partnerships (Lester and Piore 2004).

Second, because faced with this type of turbulent environment, organizations can only govern themselves effectively by experimenting, by becoming capable of learning both what their goals are, and the means to reach them *as they proceed*. To do so, as many of the relevant stakeholders as possible must take part in the *conversation*, and bring forward each bit of knowledge and wisdom that each person has, that has a bearing on the issue (Piore 1995).

The ombuds' world is one in which creative mediation is required, not only to do remedial work for the maligned party *ex post*, but ever more importantly to contribute creatively to identifying the coordination failures at the core of the governance mishaps, and to suggest the sort of organizational redesign necessary to prevent such occurrences *ex ante*. The ombuds is ideally located to do this work and to become a genuine producer of governance.

Coordination: the optimal amount of confrontation is not zero

The passage from a fully-integrated, command-and-control, hierarchical, someone-in-charge pattern of governing to a more fragmented, horizontal, collaborative no-one-fully-in-charge pattern obviously entails major coordination challenges. Governance is often defined as effective coordination when power, resources and information are vastly distributed in many different hands.

While there has been a tendency to search for coordination by shared values and consensus, and to presume that such conciliation might emerge by spontaneous generation, this is a somewhat naïve and romantic point of view. Effective coordination does not emerge organically, or without tension, except in some rare cases. Most of the time, agents and groups have quite different views of the good, and one cannot avoid confrontation in the process of mediation. Indeed, confrontation is a healthy first step in any process of change, and a steady diet of conflicts somewhat happily resolved is more likely to generate trust and better coordination (Hirschman 1995) than the distillation of *consensus mous* (i.e., vague and empty agreements).

This latter route – *consensus mous* – built on a congenital failure to confront, is most likely to generate resentment, misunderstanding and frustration, and to destroy the social capital of trust. One might easily presume that there is something like a quantity theory of angst in any organization or social system (in the way Will Self (1991) suggested that there is a quantity theory of insanity in them) and, that if one suppresses much of it in the open field, it is bound to re-emerge in other loci of the organization. So there is a great danger that, in failing to confront as a result of excessive civility or political correctness, ombuds may simply shift the problem to another locus in the organization.

Yet a long tradition of soft mediation has made confrontation somewhat unnatural for many ombuds. Indeed, there has even been a palpable culture of fear to confront, and a reluctance to proceed confrontationally with *inquiries* (a Deweyan word much preferable to the police-sounding word 'investigations') aimed at revealing unwarranted assumptions, reprehensible routines, and deep-rooted dysfunctions in organizations.

It is easy to understand why people fear to confront. One naturally fears rejection, ridicule, or potential embarrassment. Indeed, there is a social stigma attached to bullies, or persons regarded as rude, because, like Erasmus, they dare to call a fig a fig and a spade a spade. And this fear to confront is bound to grow when confrontation in a governance context is tantamount to putting into question many of the parties responsible for or connected with the organizational dysfunction, and not just one.

The result of this failure to confront is more often than not a degeneration of the inquiry into an irrational commitment to find a 'quiet resolution at all costs,' and the consequent development of *langue de bois* and *langue de coton* – meaningless discourses and wooly language aimed at making the problem disappear, rather than trying to identify its source clearly, and dealing with it frontally (Paquet 2014: chapter 5).

Failure to confront entails some form of complicity with and encouragement of the improprieties, and it is quite destructive. It ensures that bad situations endure, and that social learning is stunted. It might be defended as expedient in terms of the costs of transaction in the very short term, but the opportunity costs of such an approach in the long run are enormous, for it allows the root causes of the mishaps to remain unrevealed, and the governance repairs to remain undone. In a social context where political correctness has become a new civic religion, meek ombudsmanship may lack the appetite to proceed beyond the surface issues to the roots of the problems.

Inefficiency of bargaining

Underlining the crucial importance of conflict does not deny that conflict needs to be contained and resolved if it is to generate social learning. This can be done in various ways. But to contain and resolve conflicts, one must understand – as Geoffrey Vickers so aptly says – that "human conflict is an exercise in communication" (Vickers 1973: 146). The challenge is, therefore, to find the conditions which favour dialogue and deliberation if we want resolution and containment of conflict.

It is naïve to hope that such containment will arise as a mechanical result of the restraints of the membership, or as the result of an objective appreciation of the common situation, of an objective assessment of the expectations of others, and of an objective gauge of what individuals have learned to expect of themselves as members of the organization or society. This postulates an unbounded omniscience and a pattern of loyalty and mutual trust among the disputants that are unlikely to materialize in a world where not all disputants are hyper-rational, and where they have different notions of the good, and multiple incompatible loyalties (*Ibid*.: 148).

This explains the temptation to confront the issues head on (when one is forced to) by mimicking the game playing of the courts of law – and it is equally naïve. Wallowing in the futile search for a wholly unattainable consensus, on the basis of hard juridical principles, simply kills the urge to craft creative political compromises in response to conflicts, at the very time when such creative ombudsing is what is needed.

As Frank Ankersmit put it: "much if not all that is, (from a political point of view) new, unexpected, unforeseen, and unforeseeable will initially present itself in terms of interests not in terms of rights and legal cases. Sometimes it is only thanks to the existence of conflicts that we may become aware that something is awry and needs to be remedied" (2002: 43). The search for "compromises stimulates political creativity, consensus kills it" (*Ibid*.: 39). So, provocatively, Ankersmith argues for "principled unprincipledness" as a way to achieve peaceful coexistence in a society deeply divided on principles (*Ibid*.: 28). Ankersmith's discussion is consequential for ombuds because it debunks the seductiveness of the juridical model: he reminds his readers that a society attempting to settle juridically issues that are essentially political "may be expected to blind itself to its most urgent problems" (*Ibid*.: 43).

The inescapable road between the equally dead-endish organic emergence of consensus and juridical adjudication is bargaining. In the new world of small g governance, there has been an increasing role for bargaining. But bargaining as a process is particularly diffuse, unstructured and inefficient, as a result of "the lack of convincing equilibrium solutions and ... the incentives concerning the presentation of claims and the exploitation of power positions" (Johansen 1979: 515). There is always imperfect information, and there are incentives to supply biased information. So bargaining is often an inefficient procedure that wastes resources in the process, and fails to realize the potential gains (*Ibid.*: 519). Ombuds can do a lot to attenuate this governance failure.

The ensuing challenges for the ombuds: some hypothetical ways forward

Ombudsmanship is an old and venerable profession, and over the last few centuries it has been value-adding. But in the new small g world, the reduction of the burden of office of ombuds to curative personalized case work, or to quasi-juridical adjudication, can only lead to a trivialization of the ombuds' work – (1) either through its becoming totally ineffective as a mediation process, and incapable of creatively eradicating the sources of mishaps, or even interested in doing so; or (2) through becoming a mechanical process not unlike human rights commissions – claiming to speak for those who cannot speak for themselves, but *de facto* agreeing to uncritically become the defenders of the indefensible by accepting all claims as equally valid, putting them in a garb of rights, and thereby becoming the source of problems, rather than solutions. In both cases, the credibility of the ombuds is under threat.

The only way out of this quandary is greater depth in the inquiry process: accepting the need to tackle the issues *revealed* by the cases head-on, with the explicit intention to unearth and expose the source of the problem, and to become the architect of better governance arrangements, capable of eradicating the causes of the difficulties.

What needs to be done?

This requires the ombuds to become less passive and more active, more of an *animateur* than a moderator, a master of critical thinking, yearning to smoke out the symptoms of dysfunction, and capable of tracking down their sources and causes in a confrontational way if necessary. The core concern of ombuds should be to force both the plaintiff and the organization to face assumptions they may not be aware they are making, to contribute, through the ombudsing process, to the emergence of a *super-vision* (Innerarity 2006: 194) that defines and clarifies the nature of the problem in a manner that makes all parties see things that they could or would not be able to see by themselves – thereby teaching both the plaintiff and the organization the value of conflict.

To do so requires the ombuds to be trouble makers, persons who from the very beginning ask permission to confront, and are allowed to scheme virtuously in order to help the organization evolve (Paquet 2009a). This is the only way for ombuds to avoid being totally absorbed in the particular complaint and its idiosyncrasies, and to get at core underlying issues – what one might regard as the nature of *what the complaint reveals*. This *révélateur* dimension is what should guide the inquiry.

It might reveal nothing more than the emptiness of the charge against the organization: the misconception of a misguided complainant who has confused his/her preferences with a right or a wrong. But it may also reveal a major flaw in the governance of the organization. This revelatory work requires confronting both parties in order to generate an escape from the mental prisons that are preventing both parties from seeing the issue in its totality.

Such bringing forth of a new awareness and a new frame of reference is unlikely to emerge without much critical thinking and some confrontation. Indeed, if mediation were to ban such confrontation, it would flounder and be incapable (most of the time) of accomplishing anything but myopic and expedient obfuscation – even if the parties were happy with it. In a culture and ethos that loathe confrontation and deter it, ombudsmanship may find it difficult to generate this sort of value-adding. But if it is not done, the usefulness of the ombuds is certainly likely to be questioned.

In what way?

It is quite presumptuous for a layman to advise professionals on how to do their work. So it should be clear that this is not what is intended here. The intent is only to draw attention to *the perils of over-focalizing on the particulars of cases, without an appreciation of the context*. One can become absorbed in the minutiae and details of the idiosyncratic event as in a black hole. Escaping from this black hole is the central challenge. This can only be done by bringing both the future and the past to bear on the issue: the shadow of the future impact of the sort of resolution of the issue under consideration; and the forces of inertia buried in the history of the organization that must be considered to understand what the 'real' and fundamental sources of the difficulties have been.

This is difficult work.

On the prospective side, one wants to ensure that the future is not merrily discounted as pliable, with the unfortunate consequences of the future impact of the impending decision being disregarded in an irresponsible way. *Catastrophisme éclairé* is the name given by Jean-Pierre Dupuy (2002) to the effort to escape from this myopic and triumphalist belief that any unfortunate future consequence can be ignored because it can be corrected in due time. Making the consequences of an impending decision stark and inexorable has an extraordinarily sound impact on the generation of the *super-vision*.

On the retrospective side, it is necessary to decipher how some inexorability has grafted itself onto the organization's experience. What one is after is an historical comprehension of the dynamics of the situation. This calls for a process of reconstruction of the past, as illustrated by Jean-Marc Ferry (1996) with the use of a novel by Arturo Pérez-Reverte (*The Flanders Panel*).

This novel is developed around a painting showing a *seigneur* and a knight playing chess in full view of the chessboard – a painting produced two years after the death of the knight – on which the painter has inscribed "Who has taken the knight?" A restoration artist secures the help of a chess master to reconstruct the game from the positions of the pieces on the board in the painting. By a process of elimination of impossible moves, the chess master logically reconstructs the game and comes to the conclusion that the black queen has taken the knight.

This dual operation of making more visible the inexorabilities of the future if certain types of resolution are proposed, and of reconstructing the processes that have generated the crisis, is crucial in order to identify what is centrally important for the issue to be resolved, and what it requires in terms of modification to the governance arrangements if future catastrophic results are to be avoided.

In aid of what? – efficient bargaining, ecological rationality, and experimentalism

The new turbulent context and the new world of work generate a need for evolving arrangements if collaborative governance is to succeed. But such arrangements are unlikely to emerge unless (1) the inefficiency of bargaining is corrected; (2) some standards of ecological rationality (reasonableness, speed, domain-specific fit, matching the context) are ensured in the deliberations carried out; and (3) the requisite amount of experimentation is initiated and underwritten – by agents like ombuds who have the opportunity and the capacity to do so.

The ombuds are, through inquiries, able to correct the problems of incomplete and distorted information, of escalation of threats, and the like. Indeed, this is one of his fundamental contributions to the development of the *super-vision* that will allow all parties to see things they could not, or would not see by themselves.

The ombuds are also, through mediation and negotiation, able to guide the process of discussion, not with the view of finding the 'optimal' general solution to domain-general problems, but rather of arriving at a plausible domain-specific resolution that meets the minimal requirements of passing the test of reasonableness and matching the circumstances and environment.

At the risk of offending the sensitivity of ombuds, I would compare them (using an analogy proposed by Gerd Gigerenzer (2001: 37-50) to explain ecological rationality) to the backwoods mechanic who "has no general-purpose tool, nor all spare parts available to him. He must fiddle with various imperfect and short-range tools, a process known as 'vicarious functioning' ... He will have to try one thing, and if it does not work, another one, and with step-by-step adjustments will produce serviceable solutions to almost any problem with just the things at hand" (*Ibid.*: 43).

In so doing, the ombuds have ample opportunities to experiment. Their mandates vary considerably, and often remain relatively more fluid and open than those of other organizational agents. Yet their function has both moral authority and legitimacy, and the office holders are held in high social esteem. The office and office holders are also better equipped than most other officials to inquire in a bold fashion, and to suggest creative ways of dealing with the issues at hand. This is immensely more promising than the two alternative avenues that have tended to be in good currency of late: quasi-judiciarization and problem-elimination by empty talks.

As hinted at earlier, ombuds have much to lose by becoming too closely associated with the formal justice system, and its propensity to fall into the manichean habit of seeing everything in black and white, in terms of guilt or innocence, and not at all in terms of organizational redesign and social architecture. It equally has much to lose by becoming known as the locus where problems are simply dissolved, made to disappear and drowned in a sea of talk.

The third way between judiciarizing and sanitizing palavers focuses on the exploitation of the reconstructive work as a launching pad for the exploration of novel solutions by experimentation: prudent new ways to experiment with new collaborative mechanisms, and to improve the capacity for social learning. This calls for the ombuds to play a key role in smoothing the process of collaborative governance, through: (1) the bringing forth of contingent moral contracts as a way to make less intangible the relationships involved in collaborative governance; and (2) the learning-by-doing and doing-by-learning through which these moral contracts are continually modified as problem-handling reveals the need to do so.

Ombudsing is in the business of generating collaborative governance. Collaboration is always contingent: it is built on the tentative premise "I will if you will," and it does not crystallize instantaneously – it develops in stages. After a period of frustration, when it becomes obvious that whatever has to be done cannot be done alone, a period of experimentation driven by costs-benefits considerations becomes possible. In the second stage, building relations and close monitoring are the order of the day; and joint action is tentatively experimented with. In the third stage, increased confidence prevails, organizational memory is built, and the possibility of extending the scope of collaboration is envisaged. Demanding formal arrangements prematurely kills confidence. What is required is the development of loose, flexible and non-legally-enforceable instruments in the nature of moral contracts (e.g., memoranda of understanding and the like).

These modifiable moral contracts (Paquet 1992) serve many purposes. First, they embody some mechanism of coordination, some basis for defining agreed-upon representations, some grounds for justification, and some elements to help shape interpretation when some is needed. Second, they serve as a way to anchor, ever so loosely, the basis for monitoring and sanctioning as a foundation for social learning.

Moral contracts and conventions are deliberately elusive and flexible because they need to serve as guideposts only as long as certain circumstances prevail, and to evolve as circumstances change. This calls for *reflexive governance* – governance that constantly calls into question its own foundations in the light of changing circumstances, triggers constant problem re-definition as experience is accumulated, and even a re-configuration of the very approach to governance.

It does not pertain only to the process of self-steering, self-regulation, or self-organization, but it aims at disclosing the process of the organization's continual self-renewal and self-creation (Voβ *et al.* 2006: 4; Paquet 2005b: chapter v; Paquet 2009a).

By what means? prototyping and serious play

This is obviously a risky operation as one is entering *terra incognita*, but it would appear to be a risk worth taking, because it provides mediation with a creative and forward-looking edge.

For the time being, there is a vacuum in the whole area of organizational design: little time is spent on it, and, when it is done, it is often a job performed with extraordinary incompetence because of the poor understanding of the process of both prototyping, and serious play with prototypes, that are at the core of social learning (Paquet 2007).

The ombuds accumulate a great deal of experience through the normal activities of responding to complaints, probing different terrains, and experiencing dysfunctions of different sorts. It is possible, through such experiences (and those of colleagues worldwide) to identify the characteristics of various issues domains, of the different communities of meaning or communities of fate (i.e., assemblages of people united in their common concern for shared problems, or a shared passion for a topic or set of issues). This is enough to develop a capacity to come up with idiosyncratic workable prototypes to deal with new situations at hand.

A general template likely to be of use across the board may not be available yet, but it does not mean that a workable one cannot be elicited in the face of precise issues (Sabel 2001, 2004).

Prototyping would appear to be the main activity underpinning social learning:

- identifying some top requirements as quickly as possible;
- putting in place a provisional medium of co-development;
- allowing as many interested parties as possible to get involved as partners in improving the arrangement;
- encouraging iterative prototyping; and thereby,
- encouraging all, through serious play with prototypes, to get a better understanding of the problems, of their priorities, and of themselves (Schrage 2000: 199ff).

The purpose of the exercise is to create a dialogue (creative interaction) between people and prototypes. This may be more important than creating a dialogue between people alone. It is predicated on a culture of active participation that would need to be nurtured. The sort of playfulness and adventure that is required for serious play with prototypes is essential for the process to succeed (March 1988; Paquet 2009b: 159ff).

Yet one should not underestimate the great reluctance to experiment, to innovate, and to play with prototypes that inhabits most organizations and institutions. Most organizations have considerable capital invested in routine: any transformation is bound to expropriate the privileged positions or advantages of a number of parties. As a result, change is too often seen as a zero-sum game where everyone presumes that the only possible gains will be to the detriment of other parties. Thus, it is easy to understand why the dice are loaded against change. Very often the potential gains as a result of change remain only potentialities, while the losses are mostly obvious and measurable.

What is required is for ombuds to become agents dedicated to breaking out of this mental prison, and to transform the view of change from a zero-sum game into a positive-sum game perspective.

This opens the way to collaborative exploration and, through experimentalism, rekindles a new form of dynamic solidarity and the emergence of "experimentalist accountability" (Sabel 2004) through mechanisms of performance monitoring, comparative benchmarking, the pooled experiences of diverse and often rivalrous groups, and practical deliberations focused on the need to respond to urgent problems that call for the mobilizing of some discovery procedure (Sabel 2001).

Conclusion

For the wide-ranging family of ombuds around the world (from the one-person office already under threat, to well-established offices with a robust mandate), this invitation to subversion, and to the production of governance, is bound to be received quite differently.

Some will gauge the gamble too ambitious and dangerous; others will simply state that they are already engaged in this sort of business. Our suggestions are threatening to some and superfluous to others. The central reason for arguing in favour of such action by ombuds at this time is that there is a lack of agents of change engaged in such work in the new world of small g governance. A second reason is that there is a goodness of fit between the ombuds and this sort of job.

There is obviously a need to think through this shift of the profession's centre of gravity very carefully, for, without adequate preparation, an overly aggressive stance or an imprudent invasion of this new realm of activities could be disastrous.

The charge must be led by the more robust agencies, after careful development of their capacities as social engineers. Following that, the executive development activities, and the R&D of the professional bodies of ombuds must be altered in such a way as to help the smaller offices to gain the capacity to enter this realm of activities with some confidence. Finally, there must be a broad-based communications strategy to prepare partners and clients to accept this broader role. In particular, there will be a need to explain that this in no way threatens the conventional role of ombuds, but rather, bolsters and strengthens it by providing much additional value-adding.

The Forum of Canadian Ombuds could provide the basis for the cumulative collective intelligence and collective memory that is bound to emerge from these experiments: the experiments recorded, and their success or failures acknowledged. This would soon help all ombuds to have access to a pool of innovative experimental technologies of collaboration, prototyped and played with around the globe. Not all of those experiments will be exportable outside of their original cultural ethos, but the very process of sharing knowledge about these experiments should inspire imaginative playing with the prototypes experimented elsewhere. In practice, humans learn by refining and extending prototypes: a young child learns the word bird (by being exposed, say, to a robin) and learns to identify other non-prototypical birds by adding flats and sharps to the basic prototype. In the same manner, organizational design prototypes may be imaginatively extended to be of use in quite different and changing milieux (Johnson 1993; Paquet 2005b: chapter vii).

This transubstantiation of the ombuds role entails nothing less than a change in paradigm. Consequently, it is bound to require a revolution in the mind of practitioners: what is proposed is a change in the nature of the ombudsing business as fundamental as the revolution that carried biology from the time when animals were classified by the number of legs, to the world of DNA. For biology, this transition took a long time; in the case of ombuds, what is proposed is that it be attempted in one generation – i.e., a few decades.

For governance aficionados, the game is worth the candle. It remains to be seen if the professional ombuds will agree.

Some may regard this sort of facilitation and education mission on the road to collaborative governance as a mission impossible. They have a point. Sigmund Freud used to say that there were three impossible professions – to educate, to cure, and to govern – because they require the collaboration and the complicity of those who are supposed to be on the receiving end of the professional work. One cannot educate without explaining, or govern by decree. It can only work as processes of co-production (Innerarity 2006: 193).

Ombudsing is clearly also an impossible profession. Its contribution to collaborative governance cannot be anything less than accompanying the participants in a process of discovery that will lead them to conjure up new perspectives and identify directions that they were previously unable to see. This professional work must start, as Saul Alinsky put it, from where the world is, as it is, not as we would like it to be – working inside the system, getting people to "let go of the past and chance the future," to take a new step. It is quite difficult, for "Dostoevski said that taking a new step is what people fear most" (Alinsky 1972: xix).

References

Alinsky, Saul D. 1972. *Rules for Radicals – A Pragmatic Primer for Realistic Radicals.* New York, NY: Vintage Books.

Ankersmit, F.R. 2002. "Representational Democracy – An aesthetic approach to conflict and compromise," *Common Knowledge*, 8(1): 24-46.

Boulding, Kenneth E. 1970. *A Primer on Social Dynamics.* New York, NY: The Free Press.

Dupuy, Jean-Pierre. 2002. *Pour un catastrophisme éclairé – Quand l'impossible est certain.* Paris, FR: Seuil.

Elster, Jon. 1992. *Local Justice.* New York, NY: Russell Sage Foundation.

Ferry, Jean-Marc. 1996. *L'éthique reconstructive.* Paris, FR: Les Éditions du Cerf.

Fukuyama, F. 2004. *State-Building: Governance and World Order in the 21st Century.* Ithaca, NY: Cornell University Press.

Gigerenzer, Gerd. 2001. "The Adaptive Toolbox" in G. Gigerenzer and R. Selten (eds.). *Bounded Rationality: The Adaptive Toolbox.* Cambridge, MA: MIT Press, p. 37-50.

Grandori, Andrea (ed.). 2004. *Corporate Governance and Firm Organization.* Oxford, UK: Oxford University Press.

Gregory, R. and P. Giddings (eds.). 2000. *Righting Wrongs – The Ombudsman in Six Continents.* Amsterdam, NL: IOS Press.

Hirschman, Albert O. 1995. *A Propensity to Self-Subversion.* Cambridge, MA: Harvard University Press.

Hubbard, Ruth, and Gilles Paquet. 2002. "Ecologies of Governance and Institutional Métissage," *www.optimumonline.ca*, 32(4): 25-34.

Innerarity, Daniel. 2006. *La démocratie sans l'État – Essai sur le gouvernement des sociétés complexes.* Paris, FR: Climats.

Johansen, Leif. 1979. "The Bargaining Society and the Inefficiency of Bargaining," *Kyklos*, 32(3): 497-522.

Johnson, Mark. 1993. *Moral Imagination: Implications of Cognitive Science for Ethics*. Chicago, IL: University of Chicago Press.

Justice Canada. 2000. *Expanding Horizons: Rethinking Access to Justice in Canada*. Ottawa, ON: Department of Justice.

Laurent, Paul and Gilles Paquet. 1998. *Epistémologie et économie de la relation: coordination et gouvernance distribuée*. Lyon/Paris, FR: Vrin.

Lester, Richard K. and Michael J. Piore. 2004. *Innovation – The Missing Dimension*. Cambridge, MA: Harvard University Press.

Malone, Thomas W. 2004. *The Future of Work*. Boston, MA: Harvard Business School Press.

March, James G. 1988. "The Technology of Foolishness" in J.G. March. *Decisions and Organizations*. Oxford, UK: Basil Blackwell, chapter 12, p. 253-265.

Naisbitt, John. 1994. *Global Paradox*. New York, NY: Morrow.

Paquet, Gilles. 1992. "Betting on Moral Contracts," *Optimum*, 22(3): 45-53.

Paquet, Gilles. 1995. "Institutional Evolution in an Information Age" in T.J. Courchene (ed.). *Technology, Information and Public Policy: The Bell Canada Papers on Economic and Public Policy 3*. Kingston, ON: John Deutsch Institute for the Study of Economic Policy, p. 197-229.

Paquet, Gilles. 1996-97. "The Strategic State," *Ciencia Ergo Sum*, Toluco, MX: Universidad Autónoma del Estado de México, 3(3) 1996, p. 257-261 (Part 1); 4(1) 1997, p. 28-34 (Part 2); 4(2) 1997, p. 148-154 (Part 3).

Paquet, Gilles. 1999. *Governance through Social Learning*, Ottawa, ON: University of Ottawa Press.

Paquet, Gilles. 2000. "The Judgment of Wider Courts," Proceedings of the Symposium Expanding Horizons: Rethinking Access to Justice in Canada. Ottawa, ON: Department of Justice, p. 80-88.

Paquet, Gilles. 2005a. *The New Geo-Governance – A Baroque Approach*. Ottawa, ON: University of Ottawa Press.

Paquet, Gilles. 2005b. *Gouvernance : une invitation à la subversion*. Montreal, QC: Liber.

Paquet, Gilles. 2007. "Organization Design as Governance's Achilles' Heel," *www.governancia.com*, 1(3): 1-11.

Paquet, Gilles. 2009a. *Scheming Virtuously: The Road to Collaborative Governance*, Ottawa, ON: Invenire Books.

Paquet, Gilles. 2009b. *Crippling Epistemologies and Governance Failures: A Plea for Experimentalism*. Ottawa, ON: University of Ottawa Press.

Paquet, Gilles. 2014. *Unusual Suspects: Essays on Social Learning Disabilities*. Ottawa, ON: Invenire Books.

Piore, Michael J. 1995. *Beyond Individualism*. Cambridge, MA: Harvard University Press.

Pérez-Reverte, Arturo. 1994. *The Flanders Panel*. New York, NY: HarperCollins.

Rosenau, James N. 2003. *Distant Proximities*. Princeton, NJ: Princeton University Press.

Sabel, Charles F. 2001. "A Quiet Revolution of Democratic Governance: Towards Democratic Experimentalism" in W. Michalski *et al.* (eds.). *Governance in the 21st Century*. Paris, FR: OECD, p. 121-148.

Sabel, Charles F. 2004. "Beyond Principal-Agent Governance: Experimentalist Organizations, Learning and Accountability" in E. Engelen and M. Sie Dhian Ho (eds.). *De Staat van de Democratie. Democratie Voorbij de Staat. WRR Verkenning 3.* Amsterdam, NL: Amsterdam University Press, p. 173-195.

Schön, Donald A. 1971. *Beyond the Stable State*. New York, NY: Norton.

Schrage, Michael. 2000. *Serious Play: How the World's Best Companies Simulate to Innovate*. Boston, MA: Harvard Business School Press.

Self, Will. 1991. *The Quantity Theory of Insanity*. London, UK: Bloomsbury Publishing.

Sen, Amartya. 1999. *Development as Freedom.* New York, NY: Knopf.

Taleb, Nassim N. 2012. *Antifragile – Things that gain from disorder.* New York, NY: Random House.

Vickers, Geoffrey. 1973. *Making Institutions Work.* New York, NY: Wiley.

Voβ, Jan-Peter *et al.* (eds.). 2006. *Reflexive Governance for Sustainable Development.* Cheltenham, UK: Edward Elgar.

CHAPTER 2
| Super-bureaucrats as *enfants du siècle*: Peril I
Gilles Paquet

*"Toute découverte réelle détermine une méthode nouvelle,
elle doit ruiner une méthode préalable"*
Gaston Bachelard

Introduction

One of the most paradoxical Biblical parables, found in
the Gospel of Luke, is that of the dishonest servant who,
being asked to render account of his maladministration
to his master, anticipates that he might be dismissed. Therefore,
he assembles his master's debtors and commits forgeries which
dramatically reduce their debts. It is said that, following his
dismissal, he was held in high esteem and supported by the
debtors with whom he had conspired to rob his master, but
was also cynically appreciated by his former master for having
shown himself as a true *"enfant du siècle."*

This sacred text will serve as a starting point in an
exploration of the relationship between elected officials
(government ministers) and super-bureaucrats (Auditor
General, Chief Electoral Officer, Parliamentary Budget Officer,
agents of Parliament, and commissars of all sorts).

The members of the tribe of super-bureaucrats form a close-knit oligarchy which stems from the strong sense of superior expertise and total infallibility they would appear to share from the moment of their anointment. Yet, as one examines their work, it often reveals that these public servants appear to be agents of counter-democracy, i.e., imposing their technocratic and ideological view as the one that should prevail over that of the elected officials – whose views should prevail in a democracy.

Parliamentary democracy under attack by technocracy

According to the conventional model, senior bureaucrats are supposed to serve elected officials. If they are part of the executive arm of the government of the day, they must inform ministers to the best of their knowledge, give advice, and then proceed to carry out their minister's wishes with loyalty, imagination and creativity as long as those wishes do not run counter to the constitution and laws of the country. This model remains realistic: a large majority of senior bureaucrats fulfill this function loyally and creatively.

However, the model is being abandoned by a number of super-bureaucrats who have begun to act in ways that suggest that they interpret their mandate as being much more than simply assisting elected officials and informing the citizens.

Through a subtle (and not so subtle) mandate creep, they appear to have re-interpreted their role as monitors of certain particular dimensions of accountability as a mandate:

1. to define their own idiosyncratic interpretation of what the public interest means in their sphere of responsibility – one that may differ from the elected officials' view;
2. to proselytize this supposedly better informed perspective as superior and more legitimate than the one proposed by the elected officials; and,
3. to actively challenge, in the name of their own notion of public interest, the views of elected representatives whose legitimacy, according to them, has become questionable.

One would have expected that such 'theorizing' would be denounced by academics and the media. This is not the case. A substantial number of members of the chattering classes have celebrated this *drift from democracy toward technocracy*. Deeply persuaded of the corruption of a political system that allows all and sundry to seek to influence the government (active citizens … what a horror!), and mesmerized by the idea of a need for a transcendent, omniscient, and enlightened State, many in academe and in the media have wholeheartedly supported both the view that the superior moral authority of super-bureaucrats be recognized as uncontestable if not revered, and that they should be granted additional powers. This sort of view has percolated into the writing of columnists, and has been forcefully articulated in the academic annexes to the Gomery Commission reports (2005, 2006).

This seed of counter-democracy (Rosanvallon 2006) is one of the best guarded secrets in Ottawa. In the name of the higher interests of the country, these newly minted crusaders – agents of Parliament, commissars, and adjudicators of all types – have come to consider themselves justified in their active or passive disloyalty *vis-à-vis* their elected masters.

Fortunately, the vast majority of senior officials do not subscribe to these views. They are aware of the impropriety of such actions on the part of super-bureaucrats, and have *sotto voce* expressed critical views about this *technocratic coup d'état*, this attempt to usurp the role of elected officials as pre-eminent interpreters of the highest interests of the country.

This reaction of senior officials is understandable: it is a form of legitimate defence, since, even though super-bureaucrats have mainly directed their attacks at politicians, anyone reading their reports carefully would recognize that the *oligarchy of super-bureaucrats* has also hit hard the bureaucrats who are working in tandem with elected officials, and sometimes because they do (Heintzman 2014).

This technocratic push has received a strong support by the media who have transformed some of those super-bureaucrats into superstars – especially when they morphed into crusaders systematically attacking the government in place.

Hundreds of adjudicators are in charge of 'independent' and varied commissions of all sorts in Canada, and there are dozens of agents and quasi-agents of Parliament. All have come to be tainted to some extent by the ambient *culture of adjudication* (Paquet 2006). The presumption that super-bureaucrats are seemingly authorized to be disloyal to the elected officials (because they feel that they are better informed, and therefore better qualified to speak for the country) has also contaminated some senior bureaucrats and then some of the lower echelons of the Canadian federal public service. It has also swayed the media. For a cautionary tale about the sabotage of ministerial initiative by lower order bureaucrats, see Paquet, 2013. Given this state of affairs, some of the paranoia of the elected officials becomes understandable.

Toxic trend

This trend may have been originally triggered by the Office of the Auditor-General (OAG). After decades of serious financial accountability work complemented by benign showbiz at the time of the tabling of the AG annual report (for example, a hammer for which a small fortune had been paid, a horse on the payroll of the RCMP, etc.), there was a quantum creep of the AG's mandate that allowed it to ascertain not only whether money voted by Parliament had been spent as approved, but also to conjecture whether Canadians had had *value for money* as a result of government policy. The game moved from accounting to comparative mythologies. The AG began to question government policy (Sutherland 1999).

This is an avenue that has been followed by many other super-bureaucrats and commissars. They more or less explicitly and aggressively abandoned the traditional monitoring of existing practices to ascertain if they had been carried out in keeping with explicit legislation, and began speculating on whether such policies were in keeping with the spirit of the law (as interpreted by the super-bureaucrats themselves) and with the public interest (as gauged by whatever the super-bureaucrats claimed to have intuited). A far-reaching process of counter-democracy ensued.

The statements by crusading super-bureaucrats were echoed by academics and the media's *magistrats de l'immédiat* in denouncing government policies. Those attacks were built on a widely propagated fairy tale that purported that politicians only propose policies on the basis of *anecdotes*, while technocrats, academics and columnists base their recommendations on *evidence*. In fact, this Manichean perspective has become a mantra in some bureaucratic circles in Ottawa. Indeed, the work of the technocratic knights is being presented as the only rampart, capable of protecting citizens from the whimsical and self-interested actions of anecdote-inspired politicians.

The last decade has witnessed a swooning wave of pressures from adjudicators and super-bureaucrats to institutionalize their higher moral and legal authority. The Sheila Fraser and John Gomery tandem did much to preach this gospel, but their experience also demonstrated quite conversely how destructive the misuse of power by super-bureaucrats could be (Hubbard and Paquet 2007).

On the occasion of the sponsorship affair, revealed in mid-2000, then Auditor General Sheila Fraser theatrically declared in press conferences that the Canadian Liberal government in place "had broken all the rules in the book," (whatever this may have meant), and this statement contributed significantly to its later electoral defeat.

The Martin government was sufficiently intimidated that it created a commission of inquiry headed by John Gomery. On the basis of very lax rules of evidence and *beaucoup de conversations de taverne*, the Gomery commission came to the conclusion that accountability structures had to be dramatically overhauled, and that the power of the bureaucracy had to be increased to better monitor and constrain the behaviour of politicians.

The subsequent Conservative federal government was also sufficiently intimidated by this brouhaha that it felt it had to heed the recommendations of the Gomery commission, even though the late Arthur Kroeger and other seasoned senior bureaucrats denounced the excessive statements of the Fraser-

Gomery tandem and challenged the initiatives they suggested. The clutch of wise opponents to these initiatives did not succeed in stemming the tide of Gomery recommendations.

Elected representatives have also attempted to take measures to protect themselves from the tide of usurpation generated by the wave of counter-democracy. However, even though their counteraction was always overly timid, it was not well received. *Timid* – because of the general public opinion that had succeeded in defaming the presence of politics in public administration; *not well received* – because any proposal to rein in the usurpers met with the disapproval of a significant portion of the media and academics – who quickly accused the elected officials of censorship, or of refusing to listen to expert bureaucrats. There was also a swelling of active sabotage by other bureaucrats, who saw the possibility of parlaying this anecdote-versus-evidence fable, invented at the top, into a strategy of self-promotion at the bottom.[1] This *esprit de fronde* has translated into subterranean efforts to block, derail, or deflect the efforts of fairly able politicians (Paquet 2013). However, the full extent of the damage generated by this toxic trend might best be appreciated by capturing the deliquescence of the very notion of *burden of office of bureaucrats* that has permeated the whole of the federal public service over the last while.

It would appear that the chasm between what some lower echelon unionized bureaucrats condescend to contribute in terms of work, and what can be reasonably expected by the employer, has grown abysmal. Public servants would appear to have now come to regard any effort to reconnect meaningfully contributed work and performance expected as 'disguised discipline,' as an erosion of their status, and as nothing less than an attack on their integrity as a clergy.[2]

---

[1] For an interesting example, see Griffith (2013) for one version, and Paquet (2013) for a quite different one.

[2] A most perverse aspect of this toxic trend might be bureaucrats' refusing to recognize that the technocratic work has to be related somehow to the sort of value-adding initiatives pursued by the government. This has been observed in broad policy fields (as documented in Paquet 2013). Recently, public service

The social costs of such coordination failures engineered across the human resources regime in the federal public sector are phenomenally high, and may be ascribed in large part to the contamination of the whole political-bureaucratic interface by the fundamentalism of super-bureaucrats. A bizarre state of mind has crystallized down the whole hierarchy (a *pneumopathological state of mind* – the state of mind of those who appear morally insane, living as it were, in a fantasy-world of self-righteousness).[3] This has triggered a great amount of stubbornness and closed-mindedness in a *conflictive equilibrium situation* where neither group can get rid of the other, where both sides have to compromise, but where self-righteousness on one side blocks out any will to do so.

Additional twists

What may have obscured the real nature of this *coup* is the fact that concurrently with the mounting of these technocratic pressures, the Canadian federal government experienced a fairly dramatic transition in its political governance regime as a result of the election of a minority Conservative government in mid-2000. This came after a dozen years of Liberal domination.

Such a transition confronted bureaucrats hired, cajoled and promoted by a centre-left government with a new (maybe temporary) centre-right administration. Usually, in such circumstances, a certain natural apathy sets in, not only because the bureaucrats in place are not necessarily in agreement with the new leaders, but also because they are not necessarily likely to sense that they need to adjust to new ideas very quickly since the new ideas may indeed be only temporarily in good currency – for the minority government may fall quickly. It is in such

unions have used court action to resist even the most commonsensical requests that public servants display a modicum of engagement in their work, and in their behaviour by "showing integrity and respect; thinking things through; working effectively with others; taking initiative and being action-oriented" (May 2014).

[3] This definition is borrowed from an article by Robert Sibley published in the *Ottawa Citizen* on April 28, 2013.

a compost heap that this new dogma of the super-bureaucrat, supposedly more trustworthy than an elected representative, has been allowed to unfold.

During the early moments of the transition, trust was not high, but there was also much tolerance for glitches, and reluctance to inflict harsh punishment for what might have been perceived as deception and irresponsibility at the top of the bureaucracy. Even though a majority of senior public servants and super-bureaucrats continued to be loyally engaged in serving the government, they could not but be frustrated and discouraged by the climate of distrust which lingered on. However, who can honestly accuse the elected representatives of being unreasonably concerned when a clutch of super-bureaucrats and senior technocrats (some appointed by the new government) came to be perceived as effectively working at sabotaging the work of the new government, and when any effort to control or severely punish such disloyalty was likely to be held in contempt and sharply criticized in the media, generating much bad publicity for the government in place.[4]

Another twist has to do with ideology.

In a world marred by the epidemics of entitlements, and the profligacy by social democratic governments, the super-bureaucrats, the senior bureaucrats, and the unionized bureaucrats have found a welcoming audience by claiming to be on the side of the angels. They have propulsively engaged in persuading the citizens that any government that wishes to remind citizens that they cannot expect to receive services they are not willing to pay for is disingenuous. The groups marshaled a paradoxical dual message: government may be wasteful, but it cannot in any way reduce the size of the public service or ever replace a full-time public servant by a part-time

[4] Three urban myths have been carefully cultivated by the federal public service during this transition period: the anecdote-versus-evidence fable, the suggestion that the new government had no interest in the expert advice of the bureaucrats, and the bureaucratic clergy's claim that bureaucratic disloyalty was an oxymoron, an impossibility. These views were repeated *ad nauseam* in the media, and became regarded as conventional wisdom with little attention ever being paid to the unreality of these fictions.

one, or a public servant by an employee from the private or social sectors, without dramatically affecting the quantity and quality of services delivered to the citizens.

Utility-maximizing bureaucrats regard themselves as unabashedly progressive in the sense of using indiscriminate compassion as their legitimate reference point on the policy front. Yet defending this ideological discourse that rationalizes unbounded expenditures in the name of indiscriminate compassion is not so much as a result of a true commitment to this philosophy. It is mostly pursued because it ensures unlimited increase of the resources dedicated to the bureaucracy. They do it while denying any possibility of disloyalty *vis-à-vis* a government that has much more synoptic and less short-sighted views about fiscal policies. And when, with supporting evidence, the existence of disloyalty becomes undeniable, legions continue to insist on calling it an abominable exception, on arguing that occasional errors of judgment should be allowed, etc.

Enfants du siècle

The expression *enfants du siècle* connotes a mentality and frame of mind shaped by the culture of the century, by the ethos of the time. In our particular case, it refers to the fact that the frame of mind of the super-bureaucrats (more maybe than any other public actors) are echoes of:

1. the *moral relativism* of the time;
2. the new *self-serving rationale* of the public servants as depicted in the public choice literature;
3. the *anti-politics bias of public administration;*
4. the *pneumopathological grip* that usually seizes crusading activists and prevents them from developing synoptic and dialectical perspectives; and,
5. the self-aggrandizing tendencies of many persons elevated to a special clergy-like adjudicatory status, and tempted to abuse the discretion attached to that status.

This combination of forces does not necessarily transmogrify to the same extent all super-bureaucrats and all adjudicators, judges, commissars and the like, but all are to a degree corrupted by them – especially super-bureaucrats (Paquet 2008).

Moral relativism – stating that right and wrong are culturally relative – has created a moral no-man's land that has generated much unease especially when contradictory points of view have been in conflict. Consequently, there has been a propensity to set up institutions or loci where some determination of what might be regarded as acceptable or not on occasions of conflict. This has established a *culture of adjudication*, and the possibility for super-bureaucrats to occupy (legitimately or not) the position of adjudicator or truth-bearers in the final analysis. These potentialities have not always been explored with wisdom. Super-bureaucrats and higher court judges have often made unwarranted claims based much more on hubris than on superior competence, and couched in drama-queenesque rhetoric rather than in the sort of immensely careful language one would expect from those who have immensely great responsibilities.[5]

This hubris has also often been based on nothing more than arrogance, self-righteousness and a determination by super-bureaucrats to aggrandize their power and resource base while clothing their argument in idealistic defences of democracy and accountability. The less defendable motivations of super-bureaucrats are usually occluded by the false presumption that these individuals are always persons of exceptional clergy-like quality, entirely and exclusively dedicated to the public good. This angelic view is greatly misguided. Super-bureaucrats do not cease to work at maximizing their own utility and welfare when they get appointed (Niskanen 1968).

Another characteristic of the current ethos that has fed the delusional tendencies of the super-bureaucrats has been their antipathy toward politics that has led to ascribing to politicians

---

[5] The recent Poilievre-Mayrand exchanges about the revisions to the *Election Act* may have generated harsh language from Minister Poilievre, but it was in response to Mayrand (the Chief Electoral Officer) drama-queenesquely attacking the reform bill in its totality as "an affront to democracy" – nothing less!

all the vices and greed, while granting to bureaucrats a degree of holiness that is entirely unwarranted. This had fed the counter-democracy move (Spicer 2005).

As for the pneumopathological twist of the way of thinking of super-bureaucrats and their self-aggrandizing tendencies, this has depended much on the particular traits of individual super-bureaucrats. Many super-bureaucrats have pursued mandate creep with gusto but without zealotry, and many have used grand standing and partisan attacks to a sufficient extent that it is not unfair to refer to them not as super-bureaucrats but as partisan crusaders. In such case, the super-bureaucratic mission is less to help ensure more effective policies but rather more to embarrass the government by adopting a fundamentalist attitude and presenting whatever the government is doing as always somewhat suspect. Such crusading in garb of noble sentiments and defence of democracy betrays either poor judgment or rampant disloyalty on the part of super-bureaucrats to the elected officials.

Exception *québécoise?*

This sort of gauntlet would appear to leave very little possibility for a rebalancing of the moral contract between politicians and bureaucrats, yet, in the very portion of the country that is regarded as the most *progressive* (Quebec), there would appear to be a move toward getting rid of many of those super-bureaucrats and commissars.

In 2010, Quebec abolished some 30 of the 170 *commissions-conseils* created by earlier Quebec governments over the years (Paquet 2011). It is true that such groups did not all have the formality and moral authority of super-bureaucratic commissars, and that Quebec has made much use of commissions of inquiry of all sorts over the last decades. But there has been at least a will to disband many technocratic devices used extensively by lobbies and ideologues to press governments to act in key directions.

Since this move in Quebec was made in the name of fiscal savings, and since it left untouched the most sacred and potentially the most toxic commissions (like the one on human rights, for instance), there was no explicit debate about clipping these wings of the technocracy. Yet, it must be said that Quebec has rather firmly resisted allowing the super-bureaucrats to usurp the role of definers of the public interest – the political has firmly remained in charge of the steering function (for better or for worse), and the technocrats have never quite been able to hijack the role of *définisseurs de situation* nor to acquire the role of 'Grand Censor' of the political in the day to day affairs.[6]

Whether this administrative burp of 2010 is the expression of a will to tame the emerging impolitical, or whether it will turn out to be a quirky move without any follow-up, is not yet clear. But there seems to be more reluctance in Quebec these days to allow the usurpation of the role of the political by the technocratic.

Simple technocratic midwifery?

One of the most seductive lines of defence of technocrats, when their dominium of politicians is exposed and challenged, is to argue that they are only the *guardians of the processes* that allow the citizens to be better informed, better able to express their view, and therefore, better able to dispatch their burden of office as co-governor. This would be persuasive if not for the false assumption that super-bureaucrats are only midwives.

It may well be that a large number of bureaucrats are actively involved in maintaining the public alerted, informed, active and creative. This is a value-adding activity. But one would be wrongly advised to presume that the super-bureaucrats (and their complicit senior bureaucrats) are necessarily helping democracy to unfold more effectively and smoothly. They are often also loitering with intent in the corridors of power, and explicitly trying to substitute their notion of the public interest for the one elected officials defend. In so doing, they display much effort (and much disingenuity at times) to persuade sympathetic academics and journalists of the illegitimacy of

---

[6] This may have happened occasionally with commissions of inquiry putting the political on the defensive, but not in the way the AG and Parliamentary Budget Officer have succeeded in getting the political to live under constant threat and surveillance by the technocracy about its policy choices.

the views of elected officials, while claiming in doing so to be moved solely by their devotion to the public interest.

It is not always easy to demonstrate that super-bureaucrats can betray (and have betrayed) the trust put in them, and not lived up to their burden of office – either through mandate creep for personal aggrandizement, or through outright abuse of their office to mislead Parliament and the citizenry. Too often, when they come close to be exposed, they escape being pilloried by quick resignation from their office, when they seem to have completely used up the tolerance and culpable amnesia of Canadians in the face of such abuses.

The point here is not to document the various ways in which such abuses may occur, and the subtle ways in which they are perpetrated. This would require a full book. But two examples may be useful to make the point that such failures to meet the high demands of their burden of office do exist, are well documented, and constitute significant perils for Canadian democracy: the human rights courts and tribunals, and the Governor of the Bank of Canada – supposedly representing *la crème de la crème* of super-bureaucrats, purportedly the super-defender of the highest standards.

A casual look at Rory Leishman's *Against Judicial Activism* (2006) provides ample evidence of the malefits perpetrated by the human rights commissions and the courts with the help of the Charter of Rights. Through hundreds of pages, Leishman shows how Canadians have been held hostage to the ideologues who currently sit on our courts and human rights tribunals, and cautions that the proclivity of judges and adjudicators to make the law rather than interpret it is subverting the democratic process.

An even more invidious case is one that has tainted the reputation of the Office of the Governor of the Bank of Canada. Some will remember the deliberate misinformation concocted by the Governor of the Bank of Canada in earlier years.[7] It led to

---

[7] The personal cost borne by Gordon, as a result of his drive to expose Coyne's deception, is a cautionary tale. His original letter denouncing Coyne was signed by 29 economists, and the short book he wrote soon after demonstrated very effectively that there had been deception on the part of the Governor

the removal of James Coyne as Governor of the Bank of Canada, but it should be clear that it was only brought to light as a result of a pamphlet published by Scott Gordon (1961).[8]

The propensity to act like wicked tenants

Over time, there have always been dishonest servants. This is also true for super-bureaucrats. One may find in history public servants who have chosen to be guided by their own self-interest or ideology rather than by the public interest and the public good for all sorts of reasons. What would appear to me more poignant about the recent past is the fact that this tendency would appear to have grown both in extent and intensity (Paquet 2010).

Originally, this may have been caused by particular circumstances. After the election of the minority Conservative government in 2006, there was a period when the opposition parties were in disarray, and this created a window of opportunity for super-bureaucrats to fill that opposition gap. Indeed, the whole senior bureaucracy did not feel at first that they had to shed their old priorities since it was not clear that the minority government would be in place for long. A certain *esprit de résistance* may be said to have slowed the normal process of transition of the bureaucracy to the new regime.

For many super-bureaucrats, this was more than a transition problem. It was a window of opportunity to assert their authority by interpreting their mandate as calling for a critical appraisal

of the Bank of Canada. But after this event, Gordon was marginalized and shunned by the federal bureaucracy. His part-time career as a mediator in public service affairs was brought to a halt, and he was explicitly ignored by a royal commission later struck to study monetary affairs (even though he was one of the best known Canadian experts in this area). As a result, he chose to depart from Canada to pursue a most successful career at Indiana University in the United States. This cautionary tale illustrates the perils of exposing deception and misinformation generated by the officialdom in the public sector in Canada.

[8] Nothing would indicate that the defence mechanisms of the public sector gentility have been in any way weakened over the last 50 years: critics of the technocracy can as surely count on being ostracized, as critics of the politicians can count on being celebrated.

of the government, and by pouncing adroitly on a government that was presented, in the largely Liberal and 'progressive' media, as fundamentalist, ideological and authoritarian. It was not any longer a matter of agents of Parliament monitoring activities and reporting *ex post* on exactions, but a matter of their second guessing the choices of government, and ostentatiously demanding from government unreasonably accurate numbers *ex ante* while the very processes under review were unfolding with much uncertainty (like the war in Afghanistan or the process of workforce reduction in the federal public service).

All along, the so-called expert super-bureaucrats had no hesitation in presenting their computations as the truth, and the estimates of the government as deceitful. In so doing, not only were they delusional in declaring their arithmetical conjectures the only right ones, but they were also slanderous in declaring government estimates deceitful.

This has been done with glee in much of the last decade. It allowed the Office of the Auditor General to focus the attention of the citizenry on particularly juicy morsels of the sponsorship file in order to deflect attention from matters of greater materiality like the ineffectiveness of the Office of the Auditor General itself in detecting frauds, the toxic effect of the centralized mindset of the federal government, the growing *malaise* in the public service, to name a few. In the aftermath of the Gomery commission, accountability became the new North Star, and there was a competition amongst agents of Parliament as to who would be the more vocal a whistle-blower (Paquet 2007) not only through usual audits but even through competitive foraging of the OAG and of the PBO even in the war zone in Afghanistan!

This aggressiveness is not without reminding one of another Biblical parable, also reported in the Gospel of Luke – *the parable of the wicked tenants.*[9] In summary, it refers to a man who had planted a vineyard and rented it to some farmers. At harvest time, he sent a servant to the tenants, so that they would give him some of the fruit of the vineyard. But the tenants beat him

[9] Luke 20:9-16.

and sent him away empty-handed. After two other servants sent to the tenants were treated as shamefully, wounded, and thrown out, the owner of the vineyard sent his son hoping that the tenants would respect him. When the tenants saw him, they said "This is the heir...let's kill him, and the inheritance will be ours." So they did. It is said that then the owner of the vineyard came, killed those tenants, and rented the vineyard to others.

The new *pitbullesque* aggressiveness of super-bureaucrats has made their actions even more counter-democratic, and it is clear that the tendency to drift in this direction is likely to continue unabated since there is no mechanism to rein in those super-bureaucrats. Only self-restraint by super-bureaucrats (realizing that their super-power entails responsibility for super-prudence) would appear to be the barrier to abuses, and it is unlikely to kick in organically.

The basic culture of adjudication in Canada, and the seemingly academic reverence for the technocracy are more likely to elicit more and more of a shift from democracy to technocracy. The celebratory tribute to Kevin Page, the Parliamentary Budget Officer, in the 2013-14 edition of the creditable *How Ottawa Spends*, is very telling about where the heart of academe sits in this democracy-technocracy interface. Contrary to John Dewey's view (1935) that problems of democracy can only be solved by more democracy, it would appear that a substantial number of academics in Canada feel that the ailments of democracy can only be cured by more unconstrained technocracy.

Skepticism about technical rationality *per se* and its myopia and failures has been debated in professional circles (Schön 1983), but not so much in academe. Academe has remained much mesmerized by its imaginary, comfortable and antiquarian Newtonian world. It has not accepted that it might have to confront the quantum revolution in politics (Becker 1991). The only concession it would appear likely to make to the new quantum reality is a plea for *slower politics* i.e., a politics that remains an *être de raison* – a construct of technical rationality – uncertainty-less, bloodless, sweatless, lifeless (Heath 2014).

In this sort of world, democracy is reduced to procedural babblings and psephology ... it is a pretty desolate and mechanical fixture.

The way ahead: the sabotage of harms

The new ethos that has emerged around the so-called 'accountability of public servants in order to assure policy and program integrity and responsibilities' has created much confusion. It has opened the door to abusive interpretations that have led super-bureaucrats and some senior public servants to feel authorized to arrogate the power to decide what is in the public interest. Supported by *aficionados* in academe and in the media, this view has become viral and toxic: the citizenry has been bamboozled by this new gospel, and the foundations of democracy have been eroded.

Unless the political-bureaucratic interface is clarified anew – and the need for trust and loyalties is restated, the burden of office of the technocrats is re-affirmed as calling for active and creative support for the policies chosen by the elected government, and stiff punishment is imposed for failure to provide the best possible support – deception will thrive.[10]

Given the seriousness of the peril, priority must be given to *sabotaging the system* that generates such harms as those mentioned in the earlier parts of the paper. As Malcolm Sparrow suggests, "cleverly conceived acts of sabotage,

---

[10] These are necessary conditions (even if they are clearly not sufficient conditions) for trust to be rebuilt. Serious deliberation is required if unacceptable distortions are to be avoided. For instance, the suggestion calling for loyalty to the elected government should not be construed as condoning moral numbness and petit-Eichmannism (Bennis 1976: 54). The notion of loyalty is not an unconditional good. In the words of Joseph Tussman (1989), "loyalty is a dog without moral judgment." Public servants have a duty (as part of their burden of office) to provide their best critical advice as fully as possible to their political masters. When they have fully exercised their 'voice' option to no avail, and feel that they cannot allow themselves to be identified or associated with certain policies being implemented, and when they have given up on working patiently within the system for change, they must 'exit' and risk being an 'outsider' instead of feeling that they have a licence to deceive or a 'duty' to be actively disloyal to their political masters.

exploiting identified vulnerabilities of the object under attack, can not only be effective, but extremely resource-efficient too" (Sparrow 2008: 27). One must therefore consider a systematic offensive against super-bureaucrats and their deceitful operations.

This action has to be conducted at two levels to start with.

First, through a most effective *exposé* of the various ways in which the super-bureaucrats are abusing the discretion afforded to them. Nothing less than a quite irreverent approach will do in this work, since the major line of defence of the super-bureaucrats is built on a false image of clergy-like integrity and an expert infallibility. Excessive deference toward these institutions, excessive politeness in denouncing their excesses, and excessive political correctness preventing the generating of the required muckraking – can only amount to complicity with and moral support for the *status quo*.

Second, through some *redesign* of our institutional order (modestly but intelligently – through *bricolage*, tweaking, nudging, etc.) in order to contain the culture of adjudication, since it discourages any serious form of intelligent collaboration by offering to all parties a cop-out alternative to the difficult task of hammering out compromises. Again, a modicum of critical thinking and of irreverence is likely to be necessary to ensure that none of the adjudicatory authorities escape fundamental evaluation in the name of some imaginary and unfounded sacredness.

But sabotage must also proceed at a third-level.

A major impediment to creative and collaborative politics is the culture of adjudication underpinning the growth of the super-bureaucratic structure. This culture of adjudication is itself anchored into something surreal – an ethos of convenience and *facilité* that sweeps aside critical thinking, and sacrifices all appeal to the reasonableness of more-or-less before the altar of either-or.

The traditional old religious clergy and its supposed top-down adjudicatory duties have not disappeared. They have simply morphed into a secular authority where the source of wisdom and power is not any form of superior enlightenment but *un esprit de facilité* – an unwillingness to work hard at finding better ways, and a convenient deference to any Grand-G entity, however unwise and inept its cardinals might be, because the cost of thinking and negotiating is not zero.

The legal veneer attached to the super-bureaucratic constructions should not hide the fact that it is an emanation of what Tocqueville has called *le pouvoir social*. This is a very opaque concept that Tocqueville used regularly without feeling the need to define it precisely, but might be said to connote *conventional wisdom* in modern parlance. Raymond Boudon was more daring. He proposed the following definition:

"...the ensemble of mechanisms that impose, in a given issue domain, a dominant opinion that leads the political power to feel paralyzed (or at least forced to take it as an essential parameter in its own action), and critical thinking to be disempowered or at least more or less censored" (Boudon 2005: 168).[11]

Le pouvoir social may be ill-defined but its dynamic has underpinned many a flaky institutions and a system of beliefs in Canada, and immunized them from effective critical examination.

A good example of a flaky idea acquiring the power of a social imperative is the ideological simplification perpetrated by in the 1970s in Canada by the NDP leader David Lewis, and purporting to make it into an unassailable truth that tax relief for enterprises (put in place to stimulate innovation and improve productivity and competitiveness) is nothing more than an *unwarranted subsidy to corporate welfare bums*. It may be untrue and a grotesque misrepresentation of a reasonable state action, but it is a slogan that has been plaguing the public discourse in Canada for the last 40 years – however ill-founded, misguided and toxic such a characterization might be.

---

[11] *"...l'ensemble des mécanismes et des relais qui imposent sur tel ou tel sujet une opinion dominante devant laquelle le pouvoir politique se sent comme paralysé ou qu'il doit du moins tenir pour un paramètre essentiel de son action; devant laquelle la critique est par ailleurs impuissante, voire plus ou moins discrètement censurée"* (Boudon 2005: 168).

The toxic nature of *pouvoir social* points to the necessity of a frontal attack on the underlying ethos of convenience that underpins the culture of adjudication and the reign of super-bureaucrats, for it is unlikely that *exposé* and *bricolage* will suffice to undermine the present frame of mind in good currency in Canada. This third line of attack must aim at debunking the pneumopathological foundation for the crude philosophy of convenience and *facilité* that is at the basis of the culture of adjudication and of the super-bureaucratic institutions.

This will call for a revolution of the mind, for a reframing of our perspectives, a forceful motivation to develop *cranes* (to use the language of Richard Normann (2001: Part V) which send down a hook to lift the observer into a position where new realms are visible that could not be imagined from aground, allowing a broader and richer perspective.

This approach has been used in exploring organizational failures and design responses in private sector organizations.[12] The view from the crane is purported to have

1. *broadened* our perspective to take into account interactions (social domain), mind frames (cognitive domain), ecological and power interfaces;

2. *lengthened* our time horizon to take into account a more extended future and the possibility of learning our way out of predicaments; and,

3. *elevated* our perspective point to take into account the common public culture within which meso-organizations are nested.

---

[12] Our cranes have thrown light on five zones of tension (X-inefficiencies at the management-labour interface, escaping fault at the value-adding matrix interface, externalities at the socio-physical environment interface, hijacking at the governance interface, and moral relativism at the interface of the organization and its social and moral contexts) – zones in which much dysfunction was shown to depend on lack of trust. Pathologies were shown to be potentially corrected in part by modifications to certain necessary incentive reward systems. But even though such modifications may be necessary, they never seemed to be sufficient: fundamentally, much was shown to depend as well on developing conventions of trust and other moral contracts. The few paragraphs below have drawn freely from Gilles Paquet and Tim Ragan (2012: 108-9).

There is no standard blueprint for crane construction, but some principles have been proposed by Normann to meet the challenge of designing useful cranes. The crane must be capable of (a) taking stock of the context and of the mega-community; (b) upframing, i.e., redefining the out-boundaries of the system one is in; (c) moving boldly into future scenarios; (d) aiding in wind-tunneling any prototypes that may emerge; and (e) signaling the sort of improved competences, collaboration and design required.

In the case of the *pouvoir social* underpinning the culture of adjudication and the deference to the super-bureaucrats' world, this sort of exploration of broader horizons aims at providing a more synoptic view that can help challenge the perspectives in good currency, and open new avenues for organization design. But the ultimate aim is to destabilize both this *culture* and this *world*, and to grapple with the nebulous *pouvoir social* that would appear to give these toxic features some of their staying power. This requires laying bare the mechanisms that have been used to persuade citizens unwarrantedly to give their adherence to doubtful, fragile and utterly false ideas, and exposing them for their vacuity. One cannot see how this could be accomplished without frontally attacking the major relay mechanisms of those flawed argumentations: the media and the intelligentsia.

Conclusion

In tackling such a momentous nexus of forces, one must not allow oneself to be mesmerized by magnificent grand schemes. Inspiration must rather come from a study of the battle of the three Horatii versus the three Curiatii more than 600 years BC. As reported by Livy, at first, in the battle, the three Curiatii were wounded, but two of the Horatii were killed. The last of the Horatii, Publius, turned then as if to flee. The Curiatii chased him but, as a result of their different wounds, they became separated. This enabled Publius to slay them one by one.

Attacking frontally and directly the conventional wisdom, the culture of adjudication, and the authority of all the super-bureaucrats in place is entering a dubious battle. One might better focus on battling super-bureaucrats and adjudicators one by one, as they reveal their weaknesses ... starting with the most noxious ones.

Each of these limited battles will help in weakening or slaughtering one of these counter-democratic beasts. This is already much of an accomplishment. But as many are weakened or slaughtered, and alternative designs are imagined to deal in a more democratic way with the issues they were purporting to have under control, one may hope that some of the deeper sources of this sort of cancer might be revealed. It might then become easier to slay the rest of the bunch, and to eradicate *la source du mal*.

References

Becker, Theodor L. 1991. *Quantum Politics: Applying Quantum Theory to Political Phenomena*. New York, NY: Praeger

Bennis, Warren. 1976. *The Unconscious Conspiracy*. New York, NY: AMACOM.

Boudon, Raymond. 2005. *Tocqueville aujourd'hui*. Paris, FR: Odile Jacob.

Dewey, John. 1935. *Liberalism and Social Action*. New York, NY: Putnam.

Gomery Commission (Commission of Inquiry into the Sponsorship Program and Advertising Activities). February 2004. *Phase I Report, November 1, 2005; Phase II Report, February 1, 2006*. http://en.wikipedia.org/wiki/Gomery_Commission [Accessed November 5, 2014]. Library and Archives Canada: AMICUS No. 39208303, www.publications.gc.ca/pub?id=279898&sl=0.

Gordon, H. Scott. 1961. *The Economists versus the Bank of Canada*. Toronto, ON: Ryerson Press.

Griffith, Andrew. 2013. *Policy Arrogance or Innocent Bias? Resetting Citizenship and Multiculturalism*. Ottawa, ON: Anar Press.

Heath, Joseph. 2014. *Enlightenment 2.0*. Toronto, ON: HarperCollins.

Heintzman, Ralph. 2014. *Renewal of the Federal Public Service: Toward a Charter of Public Service*. Ottawa, ON: Canada 2020 (www.canada2020.ca).

Hubbard, Ruth and Gilles Paquet. 2007. *Gomery's Blinders and Canadian Federalism*. Ottawa, ON: University of Ottawa Press.

Leishman, Rory. 2006. *Against Judicial Activism – The Decline of Freedom and Democracy in Canada*. Montreal, QC and Kingston, ON: McGill-Queen's University Press.

May, Kathryn. 2014. "Unions Grieve New PS Performance Rules," *Ottawa Citizen*, April 7, A1-2.

Niskanen, William A. 1968. "The Peculiar Economics of Bureaucracy," *American Economic Review, Papers and Proceedings of the Eightieth Annual Meeting of the American Economic Association*, 58(2): 293-305.

Normann, Richard. 2001. *Reframing Business: When the Map Changes the Landscape*. Chichester, UK: John Wiley & Sons.

Paquet, Gilles. 2006. "Une déprimante culture de l'adjudication," *Options politiques*, 27(5): 40-45.

Paquet, Gilles. 2007. "Intelligent Accountability," a keynote address delivered at the Annual Meeting of Institute of Public Administration of Canada (Winnipeg), *www.optimumonline.ca*, 37(3): 49-66.

Paquet, Gilles. 2008. "Superbureaucrats and counter-democracy," *Canadian Government Executive*, 14(6).

Paquet, Gilles. 2010. "Disloyalty," *www.optimumonline.ca*, 40(1): 23-47.

Paquet, Gilles. 2011. "L'impasse de l'impolitique," in Miriam Fahmy (ed.). *L'état du Québec 2011*. Montreal, QC: Éditions du Boréal, p. 447-453.

Paquet, Gilles. 2013. "The Political-Bureaucratic Interface: a comment on Andrew Griffith's expedition," *www.optimumonline.ca*, 43(4): 61-74.

Paquet, Gilles and Tim Ragan. 2012. *Through the Detox Prism: Exploring Organizational Failures and Design Responses*. Ottawa, ON: Invenire Books.

Rosanvallon, Pierre. 2006. *La contre-démocratie – La politique à l'âge de la défiance*. Paris, FR: Seuil.

Schön, Donald A. 1983. *The Reflective Practitioner*. New York, NY: Basic Books.

Sibley, Robert. 2013. "Does the Canadian Governor General's wife know who's coming to dinner?" *Ottawa Citizen*, April 28.

Sparrow, Malcolm K. 2008. *The Character of Harms*. Cambridge, UK: Cambridge University Press.

Spicer, Michael W. 2005. *Public Administration and the State – A Postmodern Perspective*. Tuscaloosa, AL: University of Alabama Press.

Sutherland, Sharon L. 1999. "Bossing Democracy: The Value-for-Money Audit and the Electorate's Loss of Political Power to the Auditor General," in Richard Bird *et al.* (eds.). *Rationality in Public Policy: Retrospect and Prospect, A Tribute to Douglas G. Hartle, Canadian Tax Paper No. 104*. Toronto, ON: Canadian Tax Foundation, p. 109-140.

Tussman, Joseph. 1989. *The Burden of Office*. Vancouver, BC: Talonbooks.

PART II
New Structural Forms

CHAPTER 3

| P3 and the 'Porcupine' Problem: Initiative II

Ruth Hubbard and Gilles Paquet

"A number of porcupines huddled together for warmth
on a cold day in winter; but as they began to prick one
another with their quills, they were obliged to disperse.
However, the cold drove them together again ..."

Arthur Schopenhauer

Introduction

In Schopenhauer's parable, the animals arrive at a solution by maintaining a safe distance from one another, and as a result, while their mutual need for warmth is only moderately satisfied, they do not get unduly pricked.

In recent decades, the private, public and social/civic sectors have developed strategies of *rapprochement* and *concertation* in the name of greater efficiency, effectiveness, and economy. Indeed, public-private partnerships (PPP or P3) have been shown to reduce administrative and operations costs by some 20 to 50 percent in public transportation projects (Roy 2003). In other areas, P3s have had mixed performances: great successes, mediocre results, and major failures.

It is therefore important to understand the causes and sources of such successes and failures, and to develop the basis for some protocols that would tend to increase the probability of positive outcomes. This is a tall order for a short chapter.

Public-private partnerships – be they bipartite or multipartite – clearly pose a porcupine problem that needs to be resolved somehow. The completely different logics and mechanics of coordination that underpin private, public, and social organizations may, if properly harnessed, lead either to impressive synergies, innovation, and higher productivity, or to a good deal of waste. But to make the highest and best use of P3s, one must elicit the conditions for the best warmth/prickliness ratio.

Many have chosen to resolve the porcupine problem by walking away from it: vilifying the P3 process entirely, and damning it as fundamentally *contre-nature*. Others have uncritically embraced this new form of mixed organization, and have been in denial *vis-à-vis* the substantial evidence that it has often failed miserably. A third group (to which we belong) has felt that the benefits of P3s can be substantial, but that they cannot be obtained unless certain conditions are met.

This chapter analyzes the porcupine problem posed by P3s, and suggests a workable set of conditions that promise some value-adding, with as little pricking as possible: moderate warmth and safe distance.

Section 1 presents the basic economics and politics of the P3 process, some features of the different stages in that process, and a short primer on the centrality of well-executed contractual arrangements. Section 2 deals very briefly with the strong ideological opposition that has been mounted against such arrangements in some 'progressive' circles. Section 3 derives some lessons from our examination of a wide range of experiences in Canada and abroad, and suggests some levers that might be used to ensure a much greater probability of success for P3s. The conclusion tries to explain why the debates around P3s have been so unenlightening, and have developed such a fundamentalist tone.

The political economy and contractual nature of the P3 process

Governments cannot necessarily dispatch, solo, the complete range of tasks associated with the provision of all public or mixed public/private goods, in the most effective, efficient and economical way. Many state monopolies have come under attack for their ineffectiveness, inefficiency, and lack of innovativeness. Some forms of partnering with the private or social sectors have been shown to produce better results for taxpayers. As a result, reform-minded (and cash-strapped) governments have extended the concept of contracting out to a wider range of public activities, and significantly expanded the scope of the work done in partnership with other sectors (de Bettignies and Ross 2004).

These partnerships are hybrid arrangements that have been quite varied in terms of the targeted results, the geographical terrain encompassed, and the range of rationales of their instigators (Vaillancourt Rosenau 2000). The public activities that are involved range widely as well: from infrastructure to the re-engineering of both 'clean' services (such as civil air navigation or revenue collection) and 'dirty' ones (e.g., water, sewage and energy), to experimenting with de-institutionalizing persons with intellectual disabilities, and increasing collaboration with the voluntary or cooperative sectors on a variety of fronts.

These arrangements have been designed to take maximum advantage of the relatively better performance, for certain tasks, and of the different basic integrating mechanisms at work in the different sectors – *quid pro quo exchange* (market economy), *coercion* (polity), and *gift or solidarity or reciprocity* (community and society).

The first arrangement is based on price and non-price competition, and provides robust incentives likely to generate pressure for productivity and innovation, but may be plagued by opportunism and shirking, especially if the metering of the 'product' or of the final outcome is difficult. The coercive approach would appear to economize on coordination costs, but may lack the flexibility to adapt to local circumstances. The third family of arrangements is diffuse, and appears fragile, because it is heavily built on goodwill, but it may be most effective when trust is imperative, and the need to mobilize strong commitment matters a great deal.

P3s as a particular form of such institutional *métissage* can best be stylized from three complementary perspectives: first, as *a mega-community process* involving divergent interests and developing partnerships based on trust, in which parties may jointly pursue somewhat different objectives (Gerencser *et al.* 2006; Otazo 2006; Ramonjavelo *et al.* 2006); second, as *a number of phased activities* that go from the initial decision to enter into contractual relations with a partner or many partners, all the way through tender and evaluation, selection of partners, designing, building and operating facilities (Carson 2002); third, as *a contractual arrangement* defining the role of each party to the partnership, their duties and responsibilities, their portion of the burden of risk and of the value added generated, and the nature of the co-governance process (Kooiman 2003).

A. The first perspective draws attention to P3s as complex processes based on a mega-community – i.e., "a public sphere in which organizations and people deliberately join together around a compelling issue of mutual importance, following a set of practices and principles that will make it easier to achieve results" (Gerencser *et al.* 2006). This entails a requisite amount of both trust (institutional, inter-organizational and interpersonal) and social capital.

In practice, Gerencser *et al.* have identified four critical elements for a thriving mega-community: (1) understanding the problems to be resolved, the necessary players and partners, and the ways in which they affect one another; (2) the strong presence of partners in a listening, learning and understanding mode; (3) designing and customizing of suitable cross-sector arrangements; and (4) experiments: learning from them, and effective collective monitoring of progress.

People and groups potentially affected by, or involved in any P3, are by definition players in the mega-community. For all of them, their interests in it (and views of it) will tend to be framed by the mindset that dominates the culture in good currency in the socio-economic context. Their opinions will evolve to some extent as time passes, and will change to a greater or lesser degree as a result of external influences.

Partners have quite different expectations. In the private sector, the main interest is the profitability likely to ensue if additional efficiency and effectiveness are value adding through P3s. From the public sector point of view, even though the public good is readily invoked, bureaucrats, elected officials, political opposition, and the unionized public service may have diverse interests, and may not see things the same way. This is bound to have an impact on the nature of the negotiated contracts. The not-for-profit mindset is no more univocal. Board members, paid permanent staff, and volunteers may pursue different objectives that will shape their direct involvement and choices in P3s.

The media also play a special kind of role as opinion-moulders, to the extent that they influence the frames of reference of both the mega-community and the particular actors, and help to shape their perspectives.

B. The second perspective relates to the different phases in the construction, negotiation, and management of P3s.

The simplest representation of the array of possible arrangements is the one suggested by the Canadian Council for Private-Public Partnerships (CCPPP), which correlates the degree of involvement of private partners (but social partners may be easily added) with the degree of risk they shoulder.

This very linear and simplistic representation of the very complex P3 process has the merit of identifying a range of possibilities: from organizational arrangements where the participants are engaged in a minimal way as sheer suppliers of particular goods and services, to arrangements where the partners engage in the totality of the procurement and delivery of some public good or service, to arrangements through which the public sector completely relinquishes responsibility for the production and delivery of public services to independent private or social entities.

A more complete view would also take into account the broad social environment within which the key stakeholders are nested, the mega-community of stakeholders, and the different challenges each of the phases (from opting for P3s to the design/build/operate phase) brings forth: a high degree of understanding, trust and legitimacy in the mega-community, the choice of the right organizational form and of the right partners, the recognition that the different phases (choice of instrument, request for tenders, negotiation of the agreement, monitoring of the operations, etc.) may call for arrangements of different sorts, the right capacity to do and to learn, a rigorous management of the partnership, and some external evaluative framework capable of acting as a fail-safe mechanism (Aubert and Patry 2003).

FIGURE 2. **P3 Risk Versus Private Spectrum**

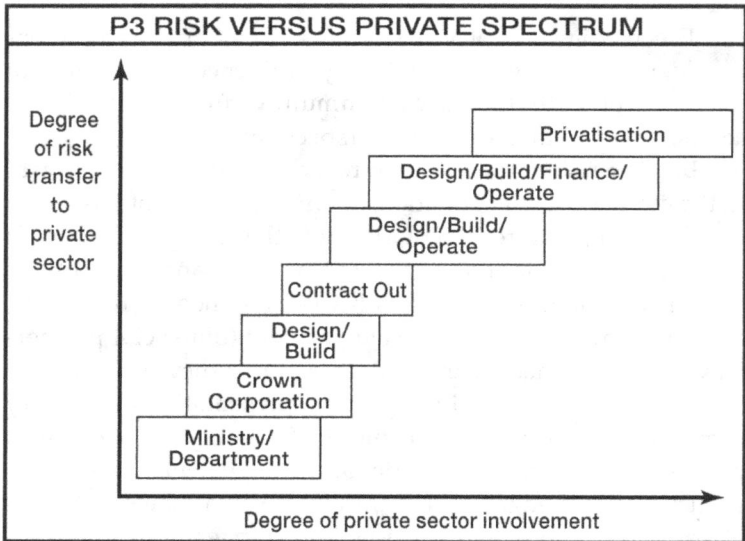

Source: The Canadian Council for Public-Private Partnerships.

A more complex representation might be that the P3 game is the combination of two sub-games.

The first is a *cognitive game* meant to provide the coordinating guidance likely to ensure as high a productivity quasi-rent as possible. This may take the form of either cost reduction and/or a better level of service. These results are meant to be achievable through a variety of ways: better incentive-reward systems and motivation, taking advantage of field experience, economies of scale, better risk management, more innovation, etc. This, in turn, generates a productivity quasi-rent – i.e., a surplus ascribable to a more effective allocation of resources.

The second is a *distributive game* meant to generate the most fruitful way of sharing the proceeds among partners, so as to ensure the viability and resilience of the arrangement.

While waste upstream is often reduced through a robust competition amongst potential suppliers, at the time of request for tenders, this does little to determine how the quasi-rent will be allocated among the partners once the contract is signed, unless these issues are explicitly addressed in the contract. The looser the arrangements, the more possibility for opportunistic behaviour there will be, and therefore the more trust that will be required.

This struggle over the sharing of costs, risks and profits generates additional costs of renegotiation/bargaining if a contract is not 'complete.' And since complete contracts are often not feasible (because of all sorts of contingencies generating instability and uncertainty that are truly not predictable), there is a substantial possibility that these additional costs will become very heavy, and that the allocation of both risks and quasi-rents will in turn generate a considerable amount of unfairness, and therefore much inefficiency.

Thus Scott Carson has underlined three important *ex ante* tests of viable P3s: (1) value-added to all partners being quite visible in the early phases of the process, and the realization by all partners that mid-stream changes are always extremely costly; (2) cost effectiveness of the time and resources used in the tendering and negotiation phases of the process; and (3) fairness in the distribution of the productivity quasi-rent and of the risks that can be expertly assessed by third parties (Carson 2002).

C. The third perspective focuses on the contractual arrangement *per se*. Its role is to ensure goodness of fit among a complex context, a diverse mega-community, intricate design-building-operations, and an effective inquiry/monitoring/learning/dispute resolution system. The nature of the contractual arrangement is meant to ensure effective, transparent, fair, legitimate and creative co-governance.

The motivations for entering into P3s may be economic and financial, managerial or strategic. For example, it may be ascribable to the fact that the public sector can no longer adequately finance all public projects (Drummond 2006). It may also be that the public sector expects to realize significant cost efficiency measures. Or it may be an attempt to shift the risk burden away from the taxpayers to the private partners. It may also be a way to cope with expertise deficiencies. More recently, there has been a deeper intermingling of public, private and civic expertise to create P3s that are focused on creating or re-engineering complex, expensive, technologically-sophisticated systems (e.g., revenue collection across several government departments and agencies).

In any of these cases, the nature of the contractual arrangements calls for negotiations by very competent experts. This has been the cornerstone for the successes of P3s in many countries: developing coherent objectives; clear delineation of inputs, risks and returns; precise definition of the responsibilities; authorities and risks; robust arrangements for risk shifting; strong and quick dispute resolution mechanisms, etc.

It entails a much stronger design, selection and contract negotiation apparatus, on the part of public sector agencies, than that which is often in place. But when such expertise is in place, in an increasing number of complex cases, joint-solution procurement (enabling the collaborative design of a wider range of options, and proceeding in stages where the measured capacity and competence of possible partners is realistically assessed) is preferred over traditional procurement in which government determines the solution to a problem and provides vendors with detailed specifications.

With regard to the most complex of these arrangements (those involving the design, building and operation of major infrastructure – bricks and mortar, or technology-rich systems), the choice is not between the traditional approach and P3, but between P3 and deferring projects indefinitely, as a result of public financial and competence constraints. Since those projects are often large in scale, capital intensive, require technical capabilities that exceed public sector capabilities, and are usually attached to identifiable revenue streams, they are initiatives that are the most amenable to P3s. It is not surprising that they have been the most popular.

Such projects – especially the bricks and mortar kind – have acquired a good reputation from some studies showing that they have been able to deliver an average savings of 17 percent, as compared to conventionally procured public sector schemes (Burleton 2006: iii). An added advantage of such P3s is that the public sector partner is usually immunized against any cost overrun in the construction phase (since it has no responsibility for it) and often immunized against cost overruns in the exploitation phase (since the revenue stream depends on the availability and use of the facilities).

Because of their long-term nature, their scope and sophistication, infrastructure projects are, however, vulnerable to miscalculations and to changes in the socio-technical context.

Consequently, contractual arrangements must ensure constant monitoring and evaluation of the process in order to detect any mishaps or flaws very quickly, and to develop a protocol to ensure that differences of opinion can be resolved quickly. This is the foundation of effective social learning (Aubert and Patry 2005; Aubert et al. 2005: 50).

Finally, there is a need to ensure that fail-safe mechanisms are in place in order to avoid sabotage, in the form of frivolous delays engineered by parties to the agreement who hope to gain from delay tactics. Such fail-safe mechanisms are meant to kick in when the usual protocols of dispute resolution fail, and if, in the view of dispassionate third parties, further delays in resolving the unresolved questions would endanger the project in significant ways. In such matters, the optimal amount of coercion in P3s is not zero.

The ideological opposition to P3s

However difficult it might be to forge the mega-community, to establish clearly and realistically that a quasi-rent really exists and can be captured, to develop the requisite capabilities and the appropriate policy and contractual instruments to do so, and to put in place the required monitoring/evaluation/ learning mechanisms to allow the arrangements to be modified smoothly as circumstances and issues evolve – the major hindrance to making use of P3s is not of a technical nature. It has to do with the ideological opposition of the chattering classes to such arrangements, an opposition that has been widely echoed in the media.

Two interesting *révélateurs* of the depth of ideological revulsion *vis-à-vis* P3s especially in Quebec are books by Boismenu *et al.* (2004) and Rouillard *et al.* (2004).

In both books (referred to hereafter as the B and R books) there is a rejection of the idea that the state might be regarded as simply *"un vulgaire prestateur de services"* (Rouillard *et al.* 2004: 86) that could contract them out in part to the private sector. Indeed, a certain Hegelian-flavoured metaphysics haunts both books: the state (always spelled with a capital S) is regarded as the fundamental societal "organism" with moral purposes that transcend those of its individual citizens (Paquet 2005).

Therefore, depending on the coefficient of Hegelianism harboured by the authors, tinkering with the state is perceived as more or less a case of *lèse-majesté*. For the 'soft' Hegelians (the B book), there is more to the state than service provision, but this does not prevent a legitimate search for more efficiency and effectiveness in alternative non-state delivery systems. For the 'hard' Hegelians (the R book), any tinkering with any aspect of the state sphere that might reduce its scope or ambit can only be regarded as an impoverishment of governance.

Both books (although to a different extent) take a particularly critical aim at the P3 component of the Charest strategy for re-engineering the Quebec state.

In the B book, the tone is skeptical. It is fairly argued that *"la montagne a accouché d'une souris"* (Boismenu *et al.* 2004: 56). The authors' view might even be interpreted as not necessarily opposed to P3s, but rather unimpressed by the way in which the Charest government is going about this strategy. There is no denial that P3s, under the right conditions, might help solve many problems, even though it is felt that the Charest government may be too timid, and that its top-down clumsiness might leave much scope for discontent and sabotage by the permanent public servants who are threatened by such arrangements.

In the R book, the tone is acerbic. The opposition to P3s is fundamental. It is asserted in a peremptory way that none of the winning conditions exist, and that none of the promises in terms of gains in efficiency and effectiveness, accountability, and quality assurance in the provision of public services can be realized. The argument in favour of P3s is chastised as *"un discours illusoire et insidieux"* (Rouillard *et al.* 2004: 108), *"une chimère"* (*Ibid.*: 115). Nothing is proved or disproved here, nor is there any need to do so: we are in the world of dogma. The attack by the R book on P3s in general is not entirely groundless. P3s are not automatically a success. Some winning conditions are necessary for P3s to work, and these are not always in place. What makes the argument somewhat toxic is that the authors presume, without any proof, that such conditions can never be realized.

The ideological underpinnings of this position are clear: if one were to allow for the possibility of such collaborative governance, the very sacred nature of the state would be eroded, and its metaphysical dominium thereby questioned – an act of heresy that cannot be entertained.

Other critics are less strident (Flinders 2005). Their comments have to do with the fact that P3s might potentially tie the hands of future governments (e.g., by requiring future contractual payments), and thereby raise challenges of accountability, transparency and legitimacy.

With respect to accountability, there is no doubt that "(d) evolving authority over decision-making and public expenditure to non-elected partnerships creates the need for new and robust forms of accountability" (*Ibid.*: 229) that may be more complex, more horizontal, and softer, and may appear less satisfactory for taxpayers.

Such concerns can be over-stated, however, and are easily repaired. Moreover, in the area of water and wastewater utilities, for example, credible observers have talked about "the myth of public sector accountability" in traditional arrangements, and said that "(w)hile municipal accountability may sound good in theory, it rarely works in practice" (Brubaker 2003: 24). There is no reason to believe that the genuine difficulties cannot be overcome by effective contracting and monitoring, together with third-party evaluation and adjudication in the case of disagreements.

With respect to transparency imperatives, the concerns are clearly over-stated: optimal transparency is not necessarily maximal transparency (Juillet and Paquet 2002) and transparency concerns cannot be allowed to trump commercial confidentiality. Some information must be kept private for legitimate business reasons. It is a matter of balance that, in most cases, can also be resolved satisfactorily by effective contractual arrangements.

As for legitimacy, there is no reason to believe that effectively, reasonably and fairly negotiated partnership contracts cannot be defended in the court of public opinion. In fact, Canadians are already on board: the Canadian Council for Public-Private Partnerships reports that six of ten Canadians (and 55 percent of public service union workers) support P3s (CCPPP 2004). Of course, not surprisingly, there is a good deal of variation in the public support by region and by type of service.

For example, support for P3s is estimated as significantly higher in Saskatchewan (three to one) than in Toronto (just over half), while it is estimated, understandably, to be lower in the field of water treatment in Ontario than elsewhere, because of the Walkerton scandal.

However ill-founded the ideological opposition to P3s may be, it has acquired legitimacy in labour unions and so-called 'progressive' and state-centric quarters. This view has been seen as especially strong in the recent debates in Quebec (Aubert and Patry 2005). It has led governments, at all levels throughout the country, to shy away or pull back from such arrangements at the first sign of controversy (Burleton 2006).

The fact that poor contractual arrangements, ascribable to incompetent negotiators, have plagued many of the early exercises in P3, has also been put to good use by P3s opponents (Mehra 2005). As a result, P3s have developed in Canada at a rate that is a great deal slower than has been the case in the UK or other European countries.

Lessons learned and winning conditions

In order to better categorize the root causes of the difficulties experienced by P3s (and consequently, to better gauge the families of prerequisites likely to be worth focusing on when attempting to ensure as high a probability of success as possible) we have stylized the overall P3 process in four modules sketched in Figure 3.

FIGURE 3: The P3 Process as Four Modules

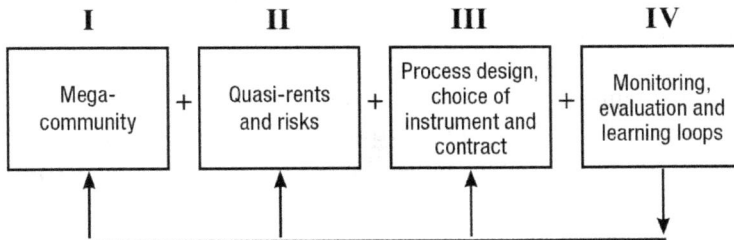

Module I pertains to the environment in which the P3 is embedded. It refers to the sort of sociological basis on which one can build: the level of trust and social capital that facilitates relationships among potential partners, the buy-in of the different stakeholders, the carrying capacity of the contextual institutions, as well as the ideological climate and the organizational culture that is present. It connotes the degree of connectivity and the organizational texture of the environment. Without a supportive infrastructure, the mega-community will not crystallize around reasonable potentialities, or will collapse with the first crisis or two.

This explains why *relational capital* is so crucial (especially at a time when potential partners, deciding whether or not to opt in, take into account things like reputation and other intangibles) and why certain often ill-informed early media reporting may poison the well and ruin the projects. It also underlines the need not only to obtain support from the mega-community at the time the project is launched, but also to maintain and sustain it with continuous action throughout the P3 process.

Module II deals with the requirement for a credible gauge of the value-adding and of the nature of the risk sharing involved in the collaborative arrangements. Even if it is not possible to foresee all the possible eventual situations that may materialize, it is essential to be able to scope the project sufficiently well that the orders of magnitude involved are relatively credible. This sort of informational base must quickly come to complement and supplement the trust capital that has allowed the partnership discussion to emerge.

If the costs, value-adding, and risks are not gauged in a reasonably accurate way, if the prospective sharing of these is not reasonably sound and perceived as fair, and if the complementary capabilities brought to the project by the different partners are not adequately recognized *ab ovo*, then again, the arrangement is unlikely to proceed very far, or to be robust.

Module III relates to the refinement of the process design and the development of contractual arrangements (both formal and informal) that will embody the contours of suitable arrangements to the degree possible (but often with strategic penumbras penciled in). This entails not only the definition of the roles and responsibilities of all parties, but also the choice of instruments, and the array of contingency plans that will kick in, in certain eventualities.

Since there is no way to write a totally complete contract envisaging all the possible eventualities, nor to presume that the rules in place will apply unambiguously to all possible circumstances, a suitable contract requires the provision for effective and rapid modification protocols and dispute resolution machinery, and some fail-safe mechanisms when all else fails. Co-governance cannot work if such mechanisms are not in place, even though they may be rarely or never used.

Module IV focuses on the central importance of continuous monitoring, including by credible third parties, effective and intelligent evaluation, and the existence of mechanisms through which the collaborative organization will learn through revising not only its instrumentalities and means, but also its objectives and broad orientation as the project proceeds, and experience reveals that the original plans might prove inadequate or less useful than had been originally anticipated, either because of changes in the environment or in the project itself.

Indeed, this fourth module feeds into the other three, and constitutes the basis of the process of social learning.

Effective social learning, that is crucial to a successful P3: (1) would enable experience to feed into the mindset of the mega-community and allow the community to transform its views; (2) would lead to a more refined and credible view of both rents and risks, and therefore to revisions of the early estimates; and (3) would allow modifications in the provisions of the contracts accordingly.

But this entails that there exist loci where the requisite discussions can be held.

One of the great weaknesses of the P3 process is a poor understanding of both the nature of such required discussions and deliberations, and the lack of the requisite places where such deliberations can be carried out. As a result, blockages quickly ensue, and viable P3s collapse for lack of safe places where the challenges generated by shocks in the environment or by unforeseen developments can be discussed, and appropriate adjustments be arrived at.

Some of this may take the form of dispute settlement or fail-safe mechanisms, but, in the main, deliberation sites must be provided on a continuous basis for the mega-community.

Unlike experts whose framework is solely technical, citizens and other members of the mega-community form opinions by integrating facts and values. P3s must presume that context and circumstances may change, and that there must be provision for people's views on tough issues to be aired and discussed, for reframing to occur, and for decisions to ensue.

Such discussions evolve through three stages – consciousness raising, reconciling proposed actions with basic values, and leaders deciding and acting to resolve the issue. A diagram (Figure 4) that Yankelovich and Rosell have used is quite useful.

Of the three stages, Yankelovich and Rosell argue that the second is the hardest, being driven less by information, and more by feelings, values and moral convictions (Yankelovich and Rosell 2001) (one might also add ideology), and it is one that people will avoid if they can. This suggests that finding effective ways to stimulate the mega-community's crystallization (with its interpersonal, inter-organizational, and institutional trust base), and then sustain it, is not going to be easy. But ignoring this social learning challenge, and hoping that all dysfunctions will fix themselves organically, is a recipe for failure over the long haul.

FIGURE 4: The Yankelovich-Rosell
Social Learning Process

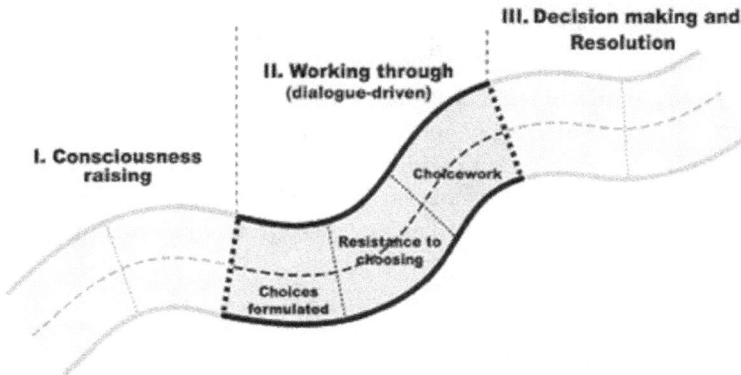

Source: www.ViewpointLearning.com (2001). This figure is no longer on the website.

If our analysis holds water, a number of modest general propositions would appear to be warranted. They do not provide the key to always-successful P3s, but they identify a number of important pressure points where effective action might be possible. One of the key differences between our list and the ones provided by other observers is that it gives more attention to context, communications and learning loops.

It has been our diagnosis that P3s have been wrongly interpreted as matters that can be handled solely through technical and legal strictures. The literature has failed to take note of the context of modern policy and regulatory development. As Carl Taylor has reminded us (1997), the development of a policy or regulatory initiatives must meet four challenges: is the proposal put forward technically feasible; socially acceptable; can it be implemented with the negotiated help of all the relevant and necessary partners; and, is it socio-politically not too destabilizing?

The undue concern with the conditions for technical and legal feasibility alone has led too many groups interested in P3s to ignore the other three challenges. This has proved disastrous in many cases.

From our point of view, the success of P3s obviously depends on sound technical feasibility and competent legal contracting, but the major sources of failure are elsewhere. The winning conditions and useful levers are mainly relational, and they require a most important capital of trust, and a most effective communication apparatus.

The eight modest general propositions that follow (two for each of the four modules identified above) are not presented as a panacea, but as a checklist that should be kept in mind (Gawande 2009). Failure on any of these fronts may be regarded as an omen of a P3 failure to come.

Proposition I-a

P3s require an aggressive, pro-active, and sustained communication strategy to ensure that all the stakeholders are fully informed and immunized against ideological hostility.

This is the fundamental requirement to ensure the crystallization of the mega-community, and the nesting of the P3 in a network of supportive relationships. It is also a way to ensure the maintenance of the trust and social capital required for the P3 to thrive. Finally, it is the only way to counter effectively the toxic effect of the interest groups' attacks on these alternative and better ways to dispatch public service.

Proposition I-b

P3s not only require effective communications, but active and creative negotiations to obtain and sustain the buy-in and active collaboration of all the key players in order to give some tonus to the mega-community.

It is one thing to obtain the *nihil obstat* of stakeholders, and quite another to engage them actively in a process of collaboration. Unless it is possible to mobilize the mega-community's capital of trust, and to negotiate the requisite moral contracts commensurate with a culture of collaboration, the P3s will not survive the first mishaps. This means that more than legal guarantees are required. It entails the development of a robust culture that will help deal with the unforeseen.

Proposition II-a

P3s must be built on credible evaluations of the value-added by the collaborative agreement.

One of the fundamental weaknesses of any P3 is the unrealistic appraisal of what might reasonably be expected from the venture. Not only do unreasonable expectations poison the relationships, but they are condemned to generating resentment and lack of credibility as results materialize, and to eroding significantly the legitimacy of the arrangement within the broader mega-community.

Proposition II-b

P3s must ensure a fair sharing of risks and profits.

The fair sharing of profits and risks is the foundation of P3s. Any arrangement based on lack of fairness can only breed distrust and disloyalty, as events reveal that the arrangement was based on deception. Whatever might have led one party to use stratagems to lure another party into a structurally unfair deal, it can only lead to a collapse of the deal and to a long-term deterioration of relations.

Proposition III-a

P3s will not succeed if it turns out that the choice of instrument was poor or if the process and the contract capturing its spirit are poorly designed.

There are important project design and legal dimensions to P3s. If a P3 is not an organizational form suitable for the task at hand, little can be done to salvage the project. In the same way, if neither the design of the project nor the legal contract is competently drawn up, P3s will crumble under their own weight.

Proposition III-b

P3s must be closely, expertly and flexibly managed.

Although the contract is the central instrument in a P3, there can never be a complete and perfect contract that has envisaged all possible contingencies. Consequently, the effective management of a P3 contract is extraordinarily important.

Project management skills are therefore essential; otherwise the arrangement is bound to founder on a mountain of minute contentions that will bring it down.

Proposition IV-a

P3s must build in the provision for credible and effective continuous external evaluation.

Whatever care is put into developing the mega-community, in choosing the right partners and instruments, in nurturing these relationships, in designing the process and contract aptly and managing it well, little can be accomplished to ensure that the P3s are on course unless care has been taken to put in place mechanisms of continuous external evaluation. This monitoring system will provide the necessary feedback to identify any mishap early, and it will be essential if social learning is to prevail. Moreover, such sources of continuous external information and appraisals will also help in guaranteeing legitimacy for the P3s in dealing with the mega-community.

Proposition IV-b

P3s also require effective dispute resolution and fail-safe mechanisms.

Despite the immense care in defining the setting and in monitoring the progress of the P3 process, disputes are bound to arise. These disputes require some external reference point or source of evaluation that can be used to bring the different parties to settle their dispute, and if no settlement emerges, some fail-safe mechanism or arbiter must be envisaged that would be empowered to ordain some form of settlement.

Conclusion

The terrain of public-private-social partnerships is plagued by the multiple meanings of the partnership label, by ideological referents, and by the paucity of meaningful evaluation of the thousands of experiments that have been carried out throughout the world (Vaillancourt Rosenau 2000; Marty et al. 2006). As a result, ideology and presumptions are having a field day.

Until such time as a richer conceptual framework is put in place, most of the case studies are simply too disparate to elicit a robust perspective on P3s. In dealing with P3s, we are still at a stage of development akin to the one in biology where animals were classified according to their number of legs.

Although no canonical set of rules is yet available that would automatically lead to successful P3s, our provisional framework may at least help to identify what would appear to be the main sources of failure. This sort of pathology of organizational forms may not be inspiring but, in this field, as in many others, it provides a *point of departure* (Paquet 2004).

Despite the fact that mixed institutions and organizations have blossomed, and that these blended institutions and organizations have often performed better than purely public or private ones, P3s are still not viewed positively. The Canadian mindset appears to be trapped in a time warp. Ever since Jane Jacobs' book (*Systems of Survival*), the Canadian federal bureaucrats, in particular, have been mesmerized by the argument put forward in this book that any form of organizational *métissage* could only generate "monstrous hybrids" (Jacobs 1992).

This *anti-métissage* theology still prevails in 'progressive' circles. Although blurring and blending have now acquired intellectual credibility (Thacher and Rein 2004), and P3s are more and more widely used at all levels of governments (and with great success) all around the world, the view remains in good currency that P3s impoverish governance because they reduce the size of the state and thereby corrupt any search for the public good.

Fortunately practice need not wait for theory to grant permission to act. We can therefore expect that the current wave of interest in using P3s will continue unabated, and that our modest general propositions (and those of others working in the field) may help to avoid a few disasters, even if they do not completely resolve the 'porcupine' problem.

However, if our central argument about the importance of the mega-community is accepted, it is clear that this is where the battle will be won: (1) by a better dissemination of information about the successes of P3s in a large number of terrains, and (2) by an effort to persuade the mega-community that it is not necessary to have a theoretical answer before engaging in an experiment. P3s may be one more case where even if the problem remains intractable in theory, it can be resolved in situated policy practice (Schön and Rein 1994: 167ff, 176).

References

Aubert, Benoît A. and Michel Patry. 2003. "Dix conditions de succès pour des partenariats public-privé," *La Presse*, December 8.

Aubert, Benoît A. and Michel Patry. 2005. "Les partenariats public-privé: le long et tortueux chemin du Québec," *www. optimumonline.ca*, 35(4): 68-74.

Aubert, Benoît A. *et al.* 2005. *Synthèse critiques d'expériences de partenariats public-privé*. Montreal, QC: Centre interuniversitaire de recherché en analyse des organisations (CIRANO), February 23.

Boismenu, Gérard *et al.* 2004. *Ambitions libérales et écueils politiques – Réalisations et promesses du gouvernement Charest*. Outremont, QC: Athéna éditions.

Brubaker, Elizabeth. 2003. *Revisiting Water and Wastewater Privatization*. A study prepared for the Government of Ontario Panel on the Role of Government, and presented at the Public Goals, Private Means Research Colloquium, Faculty of Law, University of Toronto, October 3.

Burleton, Derek. 2006. "Creating the Winning Conditions for Public-Private Partnerships (P3s) in Canada." *TD Economics Special Report*, June 22. *www.td.com/document/PDF/.../td-economics-special-db0606-p3s.pdf* [Accessed November 5, 2014].

Canadian Council on Public-Private Partnerships (CCPPP). 2004. "The People Speak on P3s: A national survey on attitudes to public-private partnerships." A survey conducted by Environics Research Group for The Canadian Council on Public-Private Partnerships, November 22.

Carson, Scott. 2002. "Establishing Public-Private Partnerships: Three Tests of a Good Process." A paper presented at the International Applied Business Research Conference, Puerto Vallarta, March.

de Bettignies, Jean-Etienne and Thomas W. Ross. 2004. "The Economics of Public-Private Partnerships," *Canadian Public Policy*, 30(2): 135-154.

Drummond, Don. 2006. "The P3-rebuilt City," *National Post*, July 26.

Flinders, Matthew. 2005. "The Politics of Public-Private Partnerships," *The British Journal of Politics and International Relations*, 7(2): 215-239.

Gawande, Atul. 2009. *The Checklist Manifesto – How to Get Things Right*. New York, NY: Metropolitan Books.

Gerencser, Mark *et al.* 2006. "The Mega-community Manifesto," *www.strategy-business.com*, August 16.

Jacobs, Jane. 1992. *Systems of Survival*. New York, NY: Random House.

Juillet, Luc and Gilles Paquet. 2002. "The Neurotic State" in G.B. Doern (ed.). *How Ottawa Spends 2002-03 – The Security Aftermath and National Priorities*. Don Mills, ON: Oxford University Press, p. 25-45.

Kooiman, Jan. 2003. *Governing as Governance*. London, UK: Sage.

Marty, Frederic *et al.* 2006. *Les partenariats public-privé*. Paris, FR: La Découverte.

Mehra, Natalie. 2005. *Flawed Failed Abandoned: 100 P3s Canadian & International Evidence*. Toronto, ON: Ontario Health Coalition (www.ontariohealthcoalition.ca).

Otazo, Karen. 2006. "On Trust and Culture," *www.strategy-business.com*, August 28.

Paquet, Gilles. 2004. *Pathologies de gouvernance*. Montreal, QC: Liber.

Paquet, Gilles. 2005. "Jean Charest's first 500 days: two anamorphoses," *Policy Options*, 26(09): 73-75.

Ramonjavelo, V. *et al.* 2006. "Une assise au développement des PPP: la confiance institutionnelle, interorganisationnelle, et interpersonnelle," *Canadian Public Administration*, 49(3): 350-374.

Rouillard, Christian *et al.* 2004. *La réingénierie de l'État – Vers un appauvrissement de la gouvernance québécoise*. Quebec, QC: Les Presses de l'Université Laval. (English version, 2006. *Reengineering the State*. Ottawa, ON: University of Ottawa Press).

Roy, Louise. 2003. "Crise des transports publics: des alternatives pour sortir du cercle vicieux," *La Presse*, December 7.

Schön, Donald A. and Martin Rein. 1994. *Frame Reflection – Toward the Resolution of Intractable Policy Controversies*. New York, NY: Basic Books.

Taylor, Carl A. 1997. "The ACIDD Test: a framework for policy planning and decision-making," *Optimum*, 27(4): 53-62.

Thacher, David and Martin Rein. 2004. "Managing Value Conflict in Public Policy," *Governance*, 17(4): 457-486.

Vaillancourt Rosenau, Pauline (ed.). 2000. *Public-Private Policy Partnerships*. Cambridge, MA: MIT Press.

Yankelovich, Daniel and Steven Rosell. 2001. Viewpoint Learning, Inc., www.ViewpointLearning.com.

CHAPTER 4
| Single-purpose Entities in the Governance of a Multiplex World: Peril II

Ruth Hubbard and Gilles Paquet

"For every problem, there is a solution
which is simple, clean and wrong ..."

H.L. Mencken

Introduction

There has been a growing tendency for governments
to respond to focalized crises (actual or imagined) by
creating single-purpose (advisory or operating) entities
to deal with them. The political rationale for such action (for
example, in the aftermath of the official languages debates
in the late 1960s, or the Gomery inquiry into the sponsorship
scandal) has been for governments to be seen as incontrovertibly
addressing the issue.

In a world that poses more and more wicked policy
problems (e.g., evolving problem definition, unclear goals,
unstable means-ends relationships, and the like), the
proliferation of these single-purpose entities (for political
optics or other reasons) has proved toxic. It has filled
the policy scene with a variety of somewhat myopic and
narrow-minded agencies. These agencies are both externally

vulnerable to being hijacked by single-issue lobbies or populist pressure groups, and internally vulnerable to becoming the nest of single-minded and/or self-righteous ideological technocracies, tending to turn them into crusading entities. Both these biases are likely to prevent them from developing an appreciative system sufficiently broad and flexible to evolve with circumstances, and to help marshal crucial trade-offs in the despatch of their mission. There has been a tendency to put the blame primarily on politicians for these aberrations, and this is somewhat unfair.

The reason these entities have proliferated is that they have received enthusiastic endorsement by a variety of groups including academics and bureaucrats absorbed by an instrumental rationalism view of public administration, and an archaic notion of public policy defined as a bow-arrow-and-target marksmanship game. For them, policy and strategy are fundamentally defined by precise goals *ab ovo*, instruments guaranteeing predictable results, and marksmanship that ensures measurable outcomes. Such a 'scientistic' and anti-politics perspective wrongly presumes that the policy maker/strategist has an actionable problem definition to begin with, abhors ambiguity, and tends to develop a propensity for technocrats to entrap real-life issues into quantophrenic boxes such as single-purpose ventures (Meier 1997).

In this chapter, we first say a bit more about the rationales behind the proliferation of single-purpose entities, and the major responsibility of experts in not having dammed that flow. Second, we refer briefly to the toxicities generated by these entities. Third, we underline the difficulties in containing these toxic effects, and in damming the irreversible damage they trigger. Fourth, since these kinds of entities are unlikely to vanish, we suggest imposing on them an inquiring system approach as a way to contain and attenuate the harms that can be anticipated from such creatures. Fifth, we illustrate the seriousness of the potential harms generated by these sorts of entities, and the usefulness of the proposed safe-fail design responses.

Political and expert rationales for such choices

Politicians are excellent at recognizing the symptoms of serious problems, and they have good reasons to propose pointed action as a very visible way of showing sensitivity to the message of those in civil society who have brought the issue forward. This kind of pointed initiative often helps to mobilize the attention of highly specialized experts who may be the source of helpful advice on the matter, and, in some cases, may act as a way to shake the inertia of the bureaucracy by creating a focal point for action considered to be a political priority.

In most circumstances, the citizen is under the false impression that all policies are the result of the government in power imposing its whims on a docile bureaucracy. In fact, most policies are the result of a very significant direct intervention from bureaucrats (and indirectly from business and other interest groups, and from academics in their consultant and teaching capacities). Bureaucrats have a central responsibility to invent and design adequate and effective policy processes likely to nudge the system in the general direction demanded by elected officials, while ensuring that the downside of such actions (if there are any) are neutralized or attenuated to the greatest possible extent.

The experts (in the bureaucracy or academe) have not acted forcefully enough to discourage the creation of single-purpose entities. They have rather wholeheartedly encouraged such initiatives as serving well their instrumental rationalism, however unwarranted and ill-advised this approach might be. The antiquarian and somewhat mechanical notion of policy in good currency in bureaucratic and academic circles wrongly presumes that the policy maker has all the information, resources and power needed to solve policy issues regarded as maze-like problems. In fact, they do **not** have all the information, resources and power to do so, and the challenges they face are not maze-like. Consequently, bureaucrats and academics have been unduly immodest and imprudent in allowing their 'scientistic' bent to overwhelm the more wholesome appreciation of politicians, and their propensity to entertain necessary trade-offs among the different relevant dimensions in this broader perspective (Spicer 2001).

Thus, instead of recognizing that wicked problems do not lend themselves to a narrow control view of policy, they have systematically comforted the politicians in the unwarranted view that the old Big 'G' (government) approach to policy making (hierarchical, centralized, authoritarian, coercive) is canonical, because policy responses can more easily be elegantly stylized with clear goals and a metrology of outcomes – the trappings of pseudo-precision and quantophrenia (Paquet 2009a). This has been argued forcefully despite the fact that, in our complex world, clear goals and measured outcomes do not necessarily amount to a meaningful way of formulating the mission envisaged – given the ill-defined state of affairs, the incomplete state of knowledge about the situation, the evolving incarnations of the problems, and the lack of commitment *ab ovo* by the partners required to do the job. Indeed, embracing such a primitive view of strategy and policy has encouraged the genesis of utopian management frameworks that have stood in the way of the job to be done, and have thereby driven a wedge between technocrats and their political masters.[1]

The toxicity of single-purpose entities

Ever since the 1980s, it has been fully realized that both more turbulent environments and a richer and more deeply diverse texture of the socio-economy have forced organizations to adjust constantly and faster in order to survive. This has created new challenges for single-purpose agencies. In fact, there has been a tendency for any such agency to take refuge in a narrowing and yet imperial interpretation of the scope of its mission in chaotic or turbulent times, in order to be able to demonstrate its value-adding contribution.

---

[1] For an oblique admission of guilt by two retired senior officials of the Canadian federal bureaucracy, see Ian D. Clark and Harry Swain (2005); for a probing of the various brands of disloyalty, of which the one mentioned here is only one, see Gilles Paquet (2010).

Over time, these single-purpose or quasi-single-purpose entities have tended to *ossify* more readily than central agencies, whose broader mandates have forced them to maintain a broader perspective in the face of on-going change, requiring a continuous modification of their operations. A good example is the difficulties of the unemployment insurance scheme in adapting to the evolution of the labour process over time (part-timers, self-employed).

In the same way, the focalization of policy action by single-purpose entities has made them an obvious target for crusading single-issue lobbies from without (e.g., minority language groups for the Office of the Commissioner of Official Languages), and made them prey to much advocacy, self-righteousness, and cognitive dissonance from within. Finally, all these factors have contributed to *stifling* the required drive to innovate and accommodate as the pace of change has accelerated.

A few examples – like the crisis around nuclear safety and medical isotopes (Hubbard and Paquet 2009) a few years back, or the hardening of human rights tribunals into fundamentalist inquisitions at a time requiring reasonable accommodations to be negotiated – are indicative of this tendency. In the first case, a worldwide medical isotope crisis was created when a Canadian nuclear safety commission that came to regard itself as handcuffed by its own interpretation of its very narrow mandate, found it impossible to engineer reasonable global versus local trade-offs when lives worldwide were endangered by its fundamentalist stand, and it forced the prime minister of the day to recall Parliament to take it out of its self-inflicted incapability. In the second case, human rights tribunals have become an abomination by falling prey to ayatollahs and illiberal ideologues, and degenerating into threats to free speech at a time when they should have evolved into negotiating tribunals, rather than becoming promoters of unreasonable accommodation (Leishman 2006).

Difficulties in containing these toxic effects

For those supporting the creation of such single-purpose entities, the standard argument has been that the convenience yield of such contraptions is high, and that they need not generate the malefits anticipated by some. Such putative malefits may be contained, it is argued, by standard and well-known constraints imposed *ab ovo* on the functioning or the structure of these entities. This is being unduly optimistic.

The possibility of containment ab ovo

Since, in most cases, these entities are created in response to wicked problems that are politically very sensitive, any attempt to firmly constrain *ab ovo* the nature of their operations would have the same effect as efforts to limit the ambit of a commission of inquiry when it is created. It would be perceived as a way of neutering the entity and preventing it from dealing freely and most effectively with the noxious problems at hand. Therefore, it would appear easier to constrain it later by various accompanying mechanisms.

a. Sunset scenario:
Limit on the life expectancy of the entities

Given the fact that a particular issue may appear to be so critical that a single-purpose entity is felt required to deal with it, one way to cope with the possibility of that entity becoming irrelevant or toxic over time is to create it as a planned non-permanent organization. The best example might be the special entity put in place to deal with the Vancouver Olympics. This is clearly an effective mechanism, but it would seem to be applicable to only a most limited sample of the cases where the single-purpose agency has been the remedy called for.

b. Conventional periodic mandate review

A less radical approach, when the problem that it is meant to tackle might be presumed to persist for an undefined period of time, is to call for a periodic mandate review of such entities to determine if they should survive, in what form, and with a similar or modified mission. Such a mandate review might suggest a termination if it is felt that the job is done, or that the task no longer needs this particular agency in charge. That is what the Quebec government did as an *ad hoc* measure in its 2010 budget, when it eliminated 30 of the 170 advisory committees that had been set up over the years (Paquet 2011). But this was done after such a long period that these committees may have had ample time to do considerable damage.

More nuanced outcomes might be provisions for a redistribution of certain functions, assessed as still useful, to existing entities with appropriate cognate missions. The mandate review might also soften the *modus operandi* of the entity somewhat (i.e., by suggesting a transformation of the way in which it carries out its mandate) in order to enable the entity to continue its work by other means. Too often, however, mandate reviews lack the gumption necessary to do anything that might appear drastic (even when it is not) as long as the issue remains ever so slightly politically sensitive.

c. Safe-fail mechanisms in times of crisis

There are moments when the narrowness of the mandate, and the drive to assert its absolute dominion over all other dimensions of the problem area, may generate some difficulty in reconciling the activities of single-purpose entities with what a broader social rationality might suggest. This would call for an *ad hoc* mediation between the entity and other entities involved in related or cognate issue domains.

In the case of administrative entities, such issues might be mediated by the Clerk of Privy Council to ensure that the entity is fully aware of the concerns of those other organizations, and that it takes these sensitivities fully into account in its decision-making process. However, the medical isotope crisis revealed that the use of the Clerk has proved a very poor safe-fail mechanism in such situations. In the case of parliamentary entities, there is no obvious locus for such mediation.

The doctrine of non-intervention

Even though the precautionary principle would suggest that all these avenues of containment be fully examined when single purpose entities are created, they are generally not explored, and even when soft safe-fail mechanisms are put in place (as the only ones politically palatable), they are not likely to be effective. This is ascribable to the sacrosanct notion of independence that is trotted out as a guarantee that the sensitive job of critical importance that led to the creation of the entity will be carried out without any sabotage (ascribable to bureaucratic morass and political interference) being allowed to derail the crusade.

This means that the worst excesses of these entities are rarely denounced, except when there is evidence of financial shenanigans or sexual misdeeds. Elected officials and the technocracy have a tendency to self-censor on this front, leaving only the media (which act invidiously as fact finder, accuser and judge) and which thrive on innuendo and insinuations, if this proves useful for their audience-building purpose (Paquet 2012a).

The mix of hands-off and *insouciance* that follows is not a matter of lack of character or professionalism; it is often a matter of fear of *lèse majesté* as a result of the special status of these single-purpose initiatives. In the case of administrative entities, the arm's length demanded from the standard ministries is always intimidating, and unless the Clerk (in the unique position of 'overlord' of all public servants) is willing to temerariously intervene, non-involvement is the default position. In the case of agents of Parliament or parliamentary entities, the *lustre* of the agency is likely to be even greater, and the arm even longer. While the prime minister and other ministers have at times been tempted to intervene, it has more often than not resulted in important political collateral damage. This has meant that there have been only oblique and indirect ways of intervening – often too late and too ineffectively to mitigate the damage.

Even more important than the formal habits and rules is the cultivation of their special character by these entities. The separate nature of these entities has acquired in the media almost the same sacred status as the separation of the legislative, the executive, and the judiciary branches of government. In the same way that a decision by a judge is not allowed to be questioned by elected officials or the executive, the same degree of reverence has come to be expected for the heads of these single-purpose entities and for their 'bulls.' Any violation of this supposedly infallible status is quickly denounced by the press, when the entity does not originate such action for its own reasons.

Consequently, there is a certain irreversibility that accompanies the creation of single-purpose entities. In the case of administrative entities, it is mostly because politicians do not dare to be seen as abandoning a cause that has gathered a large crowd of supporters; in the case of parliamentary agencies, the immunity from criticism is so deeply ingrained from within and without government that they have seemingly been granted a license to do anything they wish – however destructive.

Reframing the notions of strategy and policy

Even politicians have begun to learn from the experience of the recent past that some of these agencies can easily be hijacked by lobbies and ideologues, and can create much more collateral political damage than good. This led the Quebec government to abolish dozens of such agencies in 2010.

On the bureaucratic/academic front, there is more resistance. Public administration embodies a cosmology that is profoundly rooted in the Big 'G' ideology. Even though an alternative small 'g' approach (more pluralist, participative, horizontal and experimentalist) emerged more than a decade ago – predominantly shaped by social learning, which would appear to be better equipped to cope with the polycentric coordination challenges in our multiplex world, and more capable of yielding innovation and resilience to cope effectively with the evolving context (Paquet 1999a, b) – this alternative approach has failed to have much impact on the orthodoxy (Paquet 2012b).

Yet the toxicity of such a single-purpose agency form is such that both politicians and technocrats might be persuaded that a precautionary approach is called for. This approach might be initiated in two steps: first, by redefining policy as an inquiring system *ab ovo*, and second by better use of design thinking along the way.

An inquiring system as an alternative view of policy

This alternative approach starts from the basic position that most policy problems are ill-defined to start with, and the problem definition needs to be broached by way of an *inquiring system* that will evolve the nature of the problem as the process of probing and exploring unfolds.

At the core of this exploration is an inquiring system fundamentally seeking and processing information as a sort of self-organized, direction-finding, super automatic pilot. It is designed to mop up information; to actively seek out anomalies and investigate identifiable pathologies; to explore problem definitions; to seek out potential collaborators; to generate prototypes of responses from conversations with those collaborators; to fail early and to fail often, using these prototypes, but also to learn quickly and thoroughly from each such experimentation; to disseminate the good and bad news about what has been learned; and thereby to continuously close the knowing-doing gap within the organization or society (Hubbard *et al.* 2012: 38-39).

An inquiring system is an evolving nexus of relationships among partners and contributors that is continually being modified by the information being accumulated. Those relationships among partners are not necessarily etched in memorandums of understanding or formal partnership agreements (as some would have us believe) but in the willing co-learning and value-adding exchanges that the relationships engender. Consequently, the various relationships (internal and external, quantitative and qualitative, functional and metabolic, etc.) are continually transforming both the intelligence-gathering processes and the implementing capabilities that they mediate.

Any inquiring system is based on a cumulative process of learning and unlearning. Its outputs are appropriately compiled and acted upon through system modification, development, and redefinition over time. This learning and unlearning cycle is best facilitated by discovery engines that are frugal and flexible, that are based on learning by trial and error, and that have no guarantee of success in a world that is constantly changing. Imposing such an inquiring system framework on single-purpose entities from the start would explicitly mandate social learning as a *modus operandi*, and actions and arrangements rooted in serious play with prototypes (Schrage 2000; Paquet 2009b: 159ff).

When the unintended negative consequences of some sort of arrangements are detected, the inquiring system reacts by attempting to generate corrective action. In the same way that experiences lead organizations and social systems to modify the choice of means as the environment changes through some *level I learning loop*, the same process also operates at *level II* in modifying the goals or objectives when that becomes necessary, and at *level III* when a broader learning loop triggers a re-arrangement and a re-foundation of the organization *per se*.

Responses inspired by design thinking

Redesign is a fundamental result of the workings of the inquiring system, but there is no invisible hand generating this redesign work. It is the result of collective action, and of some collaboration among the partners mobilized by the inquiring system. But such organizational re-arrangement can only occur if the inquiring system opens the door to design thinking.

There is quite a gap between *organizational design* and *design thinking*. The former rarely avoids the trap of formulaic recipes better suited to routine repairing of ferry-boats operating between the shores of a relatively eventless river, while the latter insists on exploring ways to prepare the organization to face the turbulence of the high seas, beyond the bounds of the known (Brown 2009: 67). Design thinking prototypes from day one, and it builds on an old saying attributed to Linus Pauling about the fact that if you want to have good ideas, you must have many ideas (Linus Pauling: Wikiquotes).

In the case of single-purpose entities, both social learning and redesigning as learning proceeds need to be mandated from the start. It may be proceeding fast or slow, but, if it is mandated, the officials will have no choice but to demonstrate that they have actively taken advantage of all opportunities to intervene to tilt the inquiring system in the direction of faster social learning. This will maximize the chance that its evolutionary mission will be tackled well (Patton 2011).

Selected illustrations

Single purpose entities might not be entirely avoidable. On the other hand, no single purpose organization necessarily displays all the toxic features mentioned above, so no particular example can illustrate the perfect storm.

It would be easy to show, for instance, that a variety of entities created to accelerate the process of computerization in fields as varied as e-health or gun registration have triggered a focus on digital concerns and a displacement of the original missions. But this would tend to ascribe the whole problem to the hijacking of policy areas by technical rationality, and to occlude the fact that this is only a minor source of the problem.

The sources and causes of the malefits flowing from single-purpose agencies have less to do with technological fixations than with political and ideological shenanigans made very much easier by the hyper-focalization of such agencies, and the ease with which their activities can be derailed into fundamentalism by external and internal pressures. Indeed, the process through which such entities fall easily into premature problem definition without the necessary inquiry, and come to hyper-focus on ill-inspired superficial targets on the basis of self-righteous arguments, is a much more toxic source of the distortions that freeze the single-purpose entities into the blind pursuit of objectives regarded as sacred.

The best one can hope to accomplish in a few pages is to raise awareness of the problem by a quick look at a pair of single purpose agencies to show how they have generated some toxicity worth noting. To show how a mix of inquiring system and design thinking in their mandate might be able to do much to reduce the incidence of the malefits likely to plague such entities will be hinted at, but the bulk of the work on this front must remain a task for future papers capable of tracking down such experiments as they materialize.

The entities we have quickly looked at are the:

Canadian Nuclear Safety Commission	**CNSC**	c
Office of the Commissioner of Official Languages	**OCOL**	o

To help X-ray our illustrative cases in the simplest way, it might be useful to remind the reader of the major predicaments we have referred to in the earlier sections, and to show how the sample of single-purpose entities might be said to have suffered from some of these predicaments by mentioning them alongside with the predicament in question.

Premature problem definition	I	c
Mission: thwarted nature or mission drift	II	c o
Ossification and imperialization of the mandate	III	c o
Hijacking by lobby groups from without	IV	o
Hijacking by ideologies from within	V	c o
Flaws of conventional mandate reviews	VI	c o
Absence of an effective challenge mechanism	VII	c o

Our questioning of this sample of agencies is not meant to be an indictment, but only an expression of concern generated by our understanding of the principle of precaution, and the consequent suggestion that such agencies are prime candidates for developmental evaluation and re-foundation.

We had an opportunity to study the CNSC case in some detail elsewhere (Hubbard and Paquet 2010: ch. 11). Growing concern about the impact of nuclear energy led to the creation in 2000 of the Canadian Nuclear Safety Commission (CNSC). Its mandate is "(a) to regulate the development, production and use of nuclear energy, possession and use of nuclear substances, prescribed equipment and prescribed information … and (b) to disseminate objective scientific, technical and regulatory information to the public ..." (*Nuclear Safety and Control Act*) in order to prevent unreasonable environmental, and health and safety risks to people, and to inform the public about the effects as well as the Commission's activities.

In our opinion, the establishment of CNSC as a stand-alone entity significantly weakened the governance of nuclear energy sector. The ability to balance the risks related to people's health, safety, and the environment from the use of nuclear energy on the one hand, with the economic and social benefits that the peaceful uses that it brought here and abroad on the other, was lost.

The resulting forceful interpretation that any other considerations but safety were outside its mandate, but also were not relevant to the government of the day or the people it served (which is patently untrue), was allowed to spiral out of control with CNSC's decision to shut down a crucial reactor, thereby severely limiting the supply of urgently needed medical isotopes worldwide, and requiring Parliament to intervene to save the day.

The mission of the Office of the Commissioner of Official Languages (OCOL) is to oversee the application of the *Official Languages Act* (OLA). The OLA was originally conceived (1969) with a primary focus on ensuring that federal services were provided appropriately to the public in the official language of their choice. It was defined in the aftermath of the Royal Commission on Bilingualism and Biculturalism, and it has evolved with the 1982 Charter of Rights and Freedoms into protecting minority rights (including language rights). There was a mandate creep when the 1999 Annual Report of the OCOL determined that the "traditional watchdog role with respect to language rights has not been sufficient to fulfill the mandate" (OCOL 1999-2000) – a mandate that came to be interpreted as the enforcement of what was seen as the government's commitment to enhance the vitality and assist in the development of official language minority communities.[2]

---

[2] Office of the Commissioner of Official Languages, Annual Report January 1, 1999-March 31, 2000. As reflected in the significant 1988 amendments to the OLA reinforced by further amendments in 2005.

In tackling this aggrandized mandate, and in choosing the benchmarks for gauging community vitality – the preservation of the minority language spoken at home – the OCOL has tended to be very much at variance with the original intent of the *Official Languages Act* as understood by Pierre Trudeau,[3] and at variance with the reality of the increasing intermarriage of Francophones with non-Francophone partners.

Indeed, this choice of interpretation of its mandate – granting more importance to the traditional dynamism of conservation over the dynamism of accretion (Paquet 2008; Hubbard and Paquet 2012) (i.e., vitality measured by the capacity to attract other locutors) – might be quite consequential, to the extent that the former tradition has come to regard bilingualism as *subtractive* and not as an additional asset bolstering the community's vitality and dynamism. Community vitality and development obviously include other important factors besides the language spoken at home, and focusing mainly on this indicator may perversely shape community expectations about community vitality.

Conclusions

Our argument has been that single purpose entities are likely to be toxic in a multiplex world because they are likely to:

- simplify the problem definition process unduly, and ignore or play down significantly important trade-offs with dimensions of import that are not directly connected to a reductive version of their mission;
- fall prey to external and internal hijacking by interest groups or ideologues, and ossify and radicalize their mandate, instead of adapting it to the evolving circumstances; and,

---

[3] In fact, on tabling the first OLA, former Prime Minister Trudeau's view was clearly stated: "French Canada cannot survive by turning in on itself but by reaching out to claim its full share of every aspect of Canadian life" (Trudeau 1968). See also Supreme Court of Canada "Remarks of the Right Honourable Beverly McLaughlin, P. C., Chief Justice of Canada" (SCC 2008); and "Vitality Indicators for Official Language Minority Communities 1: Francophones in Urban Settings" (OCOL 2011).

- tend to dissociate their actions from the socio-political context within which it is nested, and elicit a fundamentalist version of their mandate in denial of the wicked nature of the problem, and of the pluralist perspective it commands.

If our argument carries any weight, it is not only a matter of acting preventively (as we suggest) when other single-purpose agencies are created, but also a matter of putting in place a massive cleansing and redesign strategy to deal with those sorts of agencies already in place, namely:

- a mandated review of all single-purpose entities, based on developmental evaluation principles, and
- some elaboration of the principles to decide what stays and what goes, and some elaboration of the principles of redesign for what stays.

The most toxic of such agencies are those which have already been institutionalized to such a degree that they have already developed a flock of subsidized lobbies vocally supporting them, or have already generated a fifth column of fundamentalists who have morphed over time into counterproductive sentinels of the past, and deniers of the realities the agencies are meant to accompany.

A developmental mandate review of all these agencies might be useful if it can be set in such a way as to avoid being hijacked (in the same manner that there are such developmental reviews for a number of legislative frameworks in many sectors, like banking for instance), but it might not suffice.

The challenges generated by single-purpose agencies must also serve as *révélateurs* of the new complexities and difficulties confronting public policy that require that the very notion of public policy be refurbished. This, in turn, calls for a revolution in the minds of bureaucrats and academics about the central importance of bringing politics back into public administration, of exorcizing anti-politics from the practice of public administration, and of frontally questioning the very flawed politics-administration dichotomy that has plagued public administration since the time of Woodrow Wilson. This point is made persuasively by Michael Spicer, and it is clearly understood by both politicians and citizens, but bureaucrats are schizophrenic about it – living in a world of explorers, but very adept at rationalizing their quest *ex post facto* so as to make it look like the result of instrumental rationalism. And academics too often remain satisfied to pronounce that the best way to find a watch lost in a dark black alley is to search for it with the help of a model teaching how to conduct a search under a lamp post because there is more light there. Consequently, we have a long way to go.

References

Brown, Tim. 2009. *Change by Design*. New York, NY: HarperCollins.

Canada. 1997. *Nuclear Safety and Control Act*. Ottawa, ON: Parliament of Canada, http://laws-lois.justice.gc,ca/acts/N-28.3/page-2.html [Accessed November 6, 2014].

Clark, Ian and Harry Swain. 2005. "Distinguishing the Real from the Surreal in Management Reform: Suggestions from Beleaguered Administrators in the Government of Canada," *Canadian Public Administration*, 48(4): 453-470.

Hubbard, Ruth and Gilles Paquet. 2009. "Design Challenges for the Strategic State: Bricolage and Sabotage" in A.M. Maslove (ed.). *How Ottawa Spends 2009-2010*. Montreal, QC and Kingston,ON: McGill-Queen's University Press, p. 89-114.

Hubbard, Ruth and Gilles Paquet. 2010. *The Black Hole of Public Administration*. Ottawa, ON: University of Ottawa Press.

Hubbard, Ruth and Gilles Paquet. 2012. "Community governance innovations: French Canada outside Quebec," *www.optimumonline.ca*, 42(3): 18-26.

Hubbard, Ruth, Gilles Paquet and Christopher Wilson. 2012. *Stewardship*. Ottawa, ON: Invenire Books.

Leishman, Rory. 2006. *Against Judicial Activism – The Decline of Freedom and Democracy in Canada*. Montreal, QC and Kingston,ON: McGill-Queen's University Press.

Meier, Kenneth J. 1997. "Bureaucracy and Democracy: The Case for More Bureaucracy and Less Democracy," *Public Administration Review*, 57: 193-199.

Office of the Commissioner of Official Languages (OCOL). 1999-2000. *Annual Report*, January 1, 1999-March 31, 2000.

Office of the Commissioner of Official Languages (OCOL). 2005. *Our History Our Path*. ww.ocol-clo.gc.ca/html/timeline/timeline_e.php?noflash=true [Accessed October 21, 2012].

Office of the Commissioner of Official Languages (OCOL). 2011. *Vitality Indicators for Official Language Minority Communities 1: Francophones in Urban Settings*. www.ocol-clo.gc.ca/html/stu_etu_sum_som_10_07_e.php, August [Accessed November 5, 2014].

Paquet, Gilles. 1999a. "Innovations in Governance in Canada," *Optimum*, 29(2-3): 71-81.

Paquet, Gilles. 1999b. *Governance through Social Learning*. Ottawa, ON: University of Ottawa Press.

Paquet, Gilles. 2008. "La vitalité des minorités linguistiques au Canada : deux perspectives," *www.optimumonline.ca*, 38(2): 30-46.

Paquet, Gilles. 2009a. "Quantophrenia," *www.optimumonline.ca*, 39(1): 14-27.

Paquet, Gilles. 2009b. *Crippling Epistemologies and Governance Failures: A Plea for Experimentalism*. Ottawa, ON: University of Ottawa Press.

Paquet, Gilles. 2010. "Disloyalty," *www.optimumonline.ca*, 40(1): 23-47.

Paquet, Gilles. 2011. "L'impasse de l'impolitique," in Miriam Fahmy (ed.). *L'état du Québec 2011*. Montreal, QC: Éditions du Boréal, p. 447-453.

Paquet, Gilles. 2012a. "Médias, imprécations et désinformation," *www.optimumonline.ca*, 42(1): 41-48.

Paquet, Gilles. 2012b. "Slouching toward a relatively stateless state," *www.optimumonline.ca*, 42(2): 99-121.

Patton, Michael Quinn. 2011. *Developmental Evaluation – Applying Complexity Concepts to Enhance Innovation and Use*. New York, NY: The Guilford Press.

Schrage, Michael. 2000. *Serious Play: How the World's Best Companies Simulate to Innovate*. Boston, MA: Harvard Business School Press.

Spicer, Michael W. 2001. *Public Administration and the State – A Postmodern Perspective*. Tuscaloosa, AL: University of Alabama Press.

Supreme Court of Canada (SCC). 2008. *Remarks of the Right Honourable Beverly McLaughlin, P. C., Chief Justice of Canada*. www.scc-csc.gc.ca/court-cour/judges-juges/spe-dis/bm-2008-02-06-eng.aspx [Accessed November 5, 2014].

Trudeau, Rt. Hon. Pierre. 1968. *Statement on the Introduction of the Official Languages Bill, October 17, 1968*. www.collectionscanada.gc.ca/primeministers/h4-4066-e.html [Accessed November 5, 2014].

PART III

New Social Technologies

CHAPTER 5

| Innovation as Redesign: Initiative III

Ruth Hubbard and Gilles Paquet

"Everyone has a plan until they get punched in the face."
Mike Tyson

Introduction

O ne of the most important impediments to innovation
is the romanticized representation of this phenomenon
that is in good currency. It is most often presented as
a glorious disruptive breakthrough by an individual genius,
when most of the time it is, in fact, the result of *bricolage* and
imaginative recombination or re-arrangement by a collective.
This romantic fabrication allows the notion of innovation to
escape into the great beyond for most of us, instead of being
presented as the daily bread of all vibrant organizations. As
a result, there has been a tendency to falsely presume that
innovation does not occur in the public sector, or to redefine
the word *innovation* so as to be able to elevate the most trivial
improvements in antiquated ways of public managing to the
status of breakthrough.

This need not be the case. Between these two extreme
sketches stands a more reasoned characterization of the process
of innovation: any significant redesign of the ways things are

done in the public sector through retooling, restructuring, or reframing. The operative word here is *significant*, defined as a non-trivial improvement of process or outcome through a meaningful redefinition of the technology in use.

In this chapter, our objective is to probe the innovation process along these lines, and to explore how innovation might be appropriately stimulated in the public sector. We proceed in four steps. First, we build our inquiry on the complementary perspectives of Brian Arthur (2009) on technology and Lester and Piore on innovation (2004) to underpin our characterization of innovation as redesign. Second, we show why, in order to deal effectively with this particular blend of technology and innovation, a shift is needed in the focus of management and governance from decision to design. Third, we provide some illustrations of successful innovations in the public sector, redescribed in those terms. Fourth, we put forward a few modest general propositions likely to be useful in the stewardship of the innovation process in the public sector.

Redefining the notions of technology and innovation

Technology and innovation are complex and contested concepts. The diverse representations of these concepts in use are too often unduly simplified, distorted or lionized. This leads to these processes – for they are processes – being bowdlerized, with the result that most studies reveal little of their true dynamics, and suggest little of use in terms of help to excite or stimulate technological change and innovative dynamics so as to make our public organizations more productive, resilient, and capable of overcoming ongoing challenges.

This section proposes clearer notions of both these processes as the only way to gain meaningful access to understanding their dynamics, and suggests a stylized definition of innovation as redesign.

Technology à la Brian Arthur

For Brian Arthur, technology is not an assemblage of practices, processes and devices, but rather a way to capture, harness and put to use *phenomena* working together for a purpose. He proposes that a technology is always organized around a central concept or principle, and around the main assembly of the device or method or process that executes this base principle. It need not be a physical device or process, but simply the idea of this device or process.

Arthur summarizes his view by stating that "novel technologies are created out of building blocks that are themselves technologies, and become potential building blocks for the construction of further new technologies...this evolution is the progressive capturing and harnessing of novel phenomena, but this requires existing technologies both for the capturing and the harnessing" (Arthur 2009: 204). From these premises, it is inferred that technology creates itself out of itself, and that "the collection of mechanical arts that are available to a culture bootstraps itself upward from few building-block elements to many; and from simple elements to more complicated ones" (*Ibid.*).

The need and demand for novel ways of doing things drive that sort of combinatorial evolution, but it does not necessarily proceed in smooth ways.

"The result is a constant rolling at all levels... new combinations appear, new technologies are added, and old ones disappear. In this way, technology constantly explores into the unknown, constantly creates further solutions and further needs, and along with this perpetual novelty... technology is not merely a catalog of individual parts. It is a metabolic chemistry, an almost limitless collective of entities that interact and build from what is there to produce new entities – and further needs" (*Ibid.*: 205).

In this view, the focus of the economy "is shifting from optimizing fixed operations into creating new combinations, new configurable offerings" (*Ibid.*: 209). As a result, it directs and mediates the evolving socio-economy but its evolution, like the evolution of technology, is "open, history-dependent, hierarchical, indeterminate and ever changing" (*Ibid.*: 205).

The complex economic system driving this evolution is an information system, providing the requisite signaling for more or less effective coordination and wayfinding, and technology may be regarded as fundamentally "an open language for the creation of structures and functions in the economy" (*Ibid.*: 25). It constantly changes the vocabularies in use.

This notion of technology is immensely broader than that which is usually connoted by this word. It covers both the material, organizational, and intellectual worlds; it pertains not only to processes and practices, but to the very ideas and principles underpinning these processes and practices; it emphasizes the fact that technologies are evolving assemblages of technologies, thereby emphasizing that technological change and innovation are the result less of a decision than of a design; and finally, and probably most fundamentally, it suggests that the combinatorial business occurs in an environment that is not merely uncertain but one where many aspects are unknown and unknowable. In such a world, "management is not to rationally solve problems but to make sense of an undefined situation – to 'cognize' it, or frame it into a situation that can be dealt with – and to position its offerings accordingly" (*Ibid.*: 210).

In this sort of world, management and governance are shifting: "from optimizing production processes to creating new combinations...from rationality to sense-making; from commodity-based companies to skill-based companies; from the purchase of components to the formation of alliances; from steady-state operations to constant adaptation" (*Ibid.*: 210).

Innovation à la Lester and Piore

Lester and Piore build their argument about the emergence of innovation on the same sense of the limitations of the problem-solving approach that postulates both that the nature of the issue is well-defined to begin with, and that the central challenge is decision making in the face of well-defined context and alternatives. They focus on the probing processes that lead to novelty, and on the fact that innovation emerges as a result of both analytical and interpretative processes. *Analytical processes* work best when alternative outcomes are well understood and well defined. But since, in fact, knowledge is always incomplete, and the range of alternatives is indeed condemned to be always poorly defined or unknown, what are most crucially required are *interpretative processes* – processes of inquiry to explore the nature of the context, the intricacies of the issues, and the range of possible, plausible, and out-of-the-box alternatives to the *status quo*.

For such interpretative work to proceed, one needs public spaces where interpretative conversations can be carried out. Such conversations are meant to feed the sort of inquiring system likely to add to knowledge through open-ended conversations among people from different backgrounds. Indeed, what emerges from such conversations is very much like the crystallization of a *language community* (Lester and Piore 2004: 11) that operates in a space of ambiguity and misunderstandings. Only by continuing to talk can the lack of comprehension be overcome.

For Lester and Piore, interpretative conversations are the mainspring of innovation. Therefore, public spaces providing a platform for such conversations are crucial contraptions, for without them, interpretative conversations are unlikely to promote:

- the questioning or the enrichment of principles in good currency;
- the harnessing of phenomena distilling new technologies and relationships;
- the serious play with prototypes; and,
- the *bricolage* designed to make the highest and best use of phenomena; etc.

Innovation as design challenge

These notions set the stage for a redefinition of the innovation process that we have sketched below. It does nothing more than spell out the sort of stylized iterative cycle through which the innovation process unfolds.

While only one loop is spelled out (when in fact a large number of iterations are always necessary before there is any convergence) and a sequencing is proposed (even though all sorts of jumping around is likely in this carousel), our sketch in Figure 5 is meant to define some sort of elementary checklist characterizing a nominal innovation cycle.

In the beginning is the issue. It may take the form of an externally-originating crisis putting some serious pressure on a public institution or organization, or a concern emerging from the financial or organizational failure of the public organization or institution, or from some strains in the environment that a public organization is trying to regulate or guide. This could be of little consequence at first, until some broader community becomes aware of the problem and begins to apply pressure for some sort of resolution. As a result, some mega-community (Gerencser *et al.* 2008) emerges that may or may not have the requisite breadth or composition to cope with the problem well. In any case, public spaces enable some interpretative conversations to be initiated (that may be kept alive or not, and nudged aptly or not by key players) that can lead to more or less effective questioning of key principles and of the technologies or ways of doing of the organization in question.

Suggestions about new combinations of principles, technologies, and relationships emerge from the varied approaches developed by the critical questioning. Interesting ideas are then pushed through the sort of filter that public policy initiatives have to go through (is it technically feasible? is it socially acceptable? is it too politically destabilizing? is it implementable?) with the help of connectors whose network spans broader public spaces.

This leads to *bricolage* (cobbling together) and redesign through experiments that may either use pilot projects or be implemented boldly. The basic issue is impacted as a result, and is often transformed by this intervention, and, after a moment, some feedback generates developmental evaluation (Patton 2011) that may reveal that the problem has been resolved or that it has been transformed into a different set of pressures that may either be less or more toxic than what existed before.

This sort of stylization leaves a number of zones less than crystal clear:

- How does the issue emerge and crystallize into a policy problem?
- How does a meaningful forum get created?
- How are interpretative conversations kept alive?
- How is the new technology (principles and ways) brought forth?
- How do the new technologies (material, organizational, intellectual) gain traction?
- How is the new technology implemented?

Much of this represents an unexplored side of the innovation process because of the lack of interest in the design process in a world where too much has been unduly characterized as mainly a problem of decision. This explains why understanding the revolution generated by a shift from a decision focus to a design focus is an important detour in our analysis.

Developing a design focus

Why

The focus on decision in traditional management and governance studies, as Boland and Collopy suggest, has led to people being completely mesmerized by a concern about choice among existing alternatives, on the assumption that the problem is already well-defined, and the possible alternatives well known. This is usually not the case. The design attitude recognizes that the problem definition has to be *constructed*, and that alternatives have to be *crafted*, and that they cannot be assumed to exist, and to be available *ab ovo*. A course of action aims at creating better alternatives than what would appear to be initially available (Boland and Collopy 2004: chapter 1; Brown 2009).

In order to deal with an approach based on exploring systems which do not exist, what is required is not only a *different attitude* that singles out these dimensions for careful attention, but also a *different vocabulary* to tackle them. Boland and Collopy have already tried their hand at a provisional version of the new sort of lexicon (Boland and Collopy 2004: chapter 37): collaboration, dialogue, improvisation, prototype, etc. These notions are essential in the designer's mental toolbox.

FIGURE 5: The Carousel of Innovation in the Public Sector

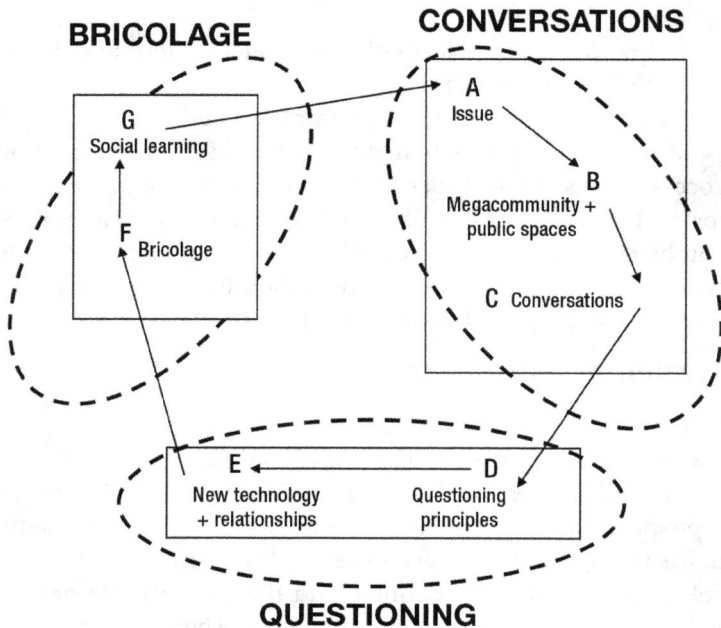

BRICOLAGE   CONVERSATIONS

G
Social learning

F
Bricolage

A
Issue

B
Megacommunity +
public spaces

C Conversations

E
New technology
+ relationships

D
Questioning
principles

QUESTIONING

In all organizations (private, public and social), the central basic challenge is a *problem definition*. Each stakeholder has his own partial definition of the problem at hand, based on his/her partial knowledge and particular interests, but these truncated views hardly suffice to define the problems at hand satisfactorily. This sort of mental prison can generate a dangerous blindness, leading to actions that are likely to be misguided when they are based on these partial, myopic, and uncertainty-denial views. Yet such views often succeed in hijacking the problem definition process, and derailing any meaningful inquiry.

What

Boland and Collopy have defined the basic elements of the design attitude that would seem to be required in our complex world. For them, "a design attitude views each project as an opportunity for invention that includes a questioning of basic assumptions and a resolve to leave the world a better place than we found it" (*Ibid.*: 9). Indeed, their 2004 book was planned to encourage a shift from a decision attitude to a design attitude.

The design attitude focuses on stewarding an inquiring system toward inventing assemblages of arrangements likely to foster better wayfinding (Paquet and Wilson 2012). To accomplish that feat, it is necessary to focus on the meso-level.

Organizations and institutions are meso-phenomena, too often poorly described and apprehended, because observers insist on looking at them through micro-perspectives that focus exclusively on individual entities as absolutes, and deny the importance of relationships between entities. They are equally poorly understood by approaches focusing exclusively on macro-systems and totalities as absolutes. Organizational design requires a vocabulary and an approach that focus at the meso-level.

How

The new competencies and skills that need to be developed have much to do with *savoir-faire*, *savoir-être* (personal development), and learning by doing. Such competencies, based on practical knowledge, have tended to be greatly underrated in a world where technical rationality has wrongly become hegemonic:

presuming that knowledge flows only one way – from underlying disciplines to applied science to actual performance of services to clients and society.

Organizational design uses a variety of mechanisms to help institute a living organization that has the capacity to be reliable but innovative, and to be resilient but to learn. It aims at coherence, but mainly at dynamism. This cannot be accomplished by tinkering only with the hard dimensions of organizations (architecture and routines); it must also modify the soft dimensions (behaviour and culture).

This is an especially daunting task as the designer is always confronted with trade-offs between exploiting existing knowledge, or exploring for new knowledge, when having to meet the dual challenge of reliability and innovation (March 1991). It is often impossible to tackle this sort of challenge without modifying the culture of the organization, for it may be incapable of accomplishing such a feat.

Some principles have proven useful in this sort of work (Paquet 2005: chapter 8):

- maximum participation to ensure tapping into all relevant knowledge and more collaboration;
- subsidiarity, or the delegation of decision making to the most local level possible;
- some competition to squeeze out organizational slack and promote innovation; and,
- multi-stability, i.e., the partitioning of the organization into sub-systems, so as to be able to delegate to the one most able to handle a shock or perturbation the task of doing so, without the other sub-systems being forced to transform.

As for the most useful mechanisms, they have been:

- the setting up of ever more inclusive forums for effective multilogue;
- the negotiation of moral contracts, defining clearly and well, yet informally, the mutual expectations of the different partners;
- the design of learning loops, enabling the partners to revise their choices of means as the experience unfolds, but also

to revise the very ends pursued through reframing the organization when it proves necessary; and,

• the invention of fail-safe mechanisms to ensure that the multilogue does not degenerate into meaningless consensuses, and to prevent *saboteurs* from derailing the collective effort.

The designer must be ready to prototype and to tinker as the process unfolds, but no organization will permit that unless some sense of the nature of the experiment action plan is first at least hinted at.

Scoping design thinking

In 2004, Karl Weick published a paper in which he rooted his reflections on rethinking organizational design in the examination of the testimonies of two well-known designers: Frank Gehry (the famous architect) and Dee Hock (the ex-CEO who designed VISA) (Weick 2004: 36-53; Gehry 1999; Hock 1999) – both blessed with an uncanny ability at such work. The main lesson Weick drew from these reflections is that even though coordination is a central concern of designers – the job of generating contraptions that not only reconcile the pressures from the geo-technical constraints and from the values and plans of the various stakeholders, but also the job of coordinating the activities of all those who have a significant portion of the information, resources, and power that need to be mobilized to ensure resilience and innovation – there is a danger that allowing a fixation on some rigid and impatient coordination imperative might impair the whole design process.

Weick quotes Dee Hock as observing that management is unduly focused on creating "constants, uniformity and efficiency," when what is required in our turbulent world is to understand and coordinate "variability, complexity, and effectiveness." Weick suggests that these modern requirements identified by Hock "are best achieved if design is recast as designing that uses transient constructs, *bricolage*, and improvisation" (Weick 2004: 47).

This emphasis on on-going and living processes has a Deweyian flavour: John Dewey always refused to use terms with static connotation, like thing or object, to connote human realities and activities. He preferred using the more elusive notion of *affairs*. In the words of a Dewey scholar, "affairs are never frozen, finished or complete. They form a world characterized by genuine contingency and continual process. A world of affairs is a world of actualities open to a variety of possibilities" (Boisvert 1998: 24).

Therefore, for Weick and others, *one must design for transience and incompleteness*: being satisfied to define the skeleton or bare bones framework, and to allow an emergent structure to develop around it as partners interact, argue, come together and learn along the way. This is exactly what Gehry and Hock would appear to have been doing.

One interesting way in which the new attitude might be generated has been presented in Weick and Sutcliffe's *Managing the Unexpected* (2007). They have identified principles guiding high-reliability organizations in the face of turbulent environments. Three of these principles help to improve sensitivity and capacity to react quickly to the unexpected, and two of them have to do with the capacity to contain the toxic impacts of these avalanches:

- preoccupation with failure;
- reluctance to simplify;
- sensitivity to operations;
- commitment to resilience; and,
- deference to expertise.

These principles are built on *mindfulness*.

Weick and Sutcliffe have shown that these capabilities may be nudged into becoming instituted into the organizational culture, and may be managed through leveraging 'small wins' into progress of the organizational culture toward greater mindfulness.

Innovations as redesign: some illustrations

In order to illustrate how the new approach is not only workable, but that it corresponds to what has been observed in certain important organizational innovations that have been celebrated of late in the public sector, we proceed in two stages.

First, we provide some synthetic background information about the three basic phases of the innovation carousel in the two case studies, with particular attention to the simplicity of the Resto Project case (simple retooling), and the greater complexity of the forestry case (restructuring and reframing that have unfolded simultaneously at two levels – the level of a particular government agency, and the level of the industry as a whole).

Second, we show how in each of the two cases many of the elements underlined in our general framework are featured.

Two projects elliptically described

To fix ideas, we have summarized first the main features of the two case studies in a most elliptical way in Table 1. The rest of the section fleshes out the main features of the innovation process along the lines suggested by the innovation cycle or carousel discussed above.

Resto Project
Conversations
Tax evasion and under-the-table work is of particular concern in the restaurant and construction sectors in Quebec, because it causes serious loss of revenue to the provincial government, and results in unfair competition for businesses operating above board. In the restaurant sector, Revenue Québec (RQ) losses were estimated to be something like $419M/year.

The Resto Project on "mandatory billing in the restaurant sector in Quebec" (Revenue Québec 2012: 2), required restaurant owners to report their real sales figures, and remit all taxes paid by their patrons through a new technological arrangement.

TABLE 1: Features of The Two Innovation Processes

Cases	Resto Project	Forest industry	
		In the large	In the small
Carousel issue	• Tax evasion • Unfair competition	• International competition	
Public spaces	• 200-400 RO people • IBM Canada • 5 restaurateur associations • 5 restaurateur associations • installers, developer / manufacturer of sales recording systems	• Canadian Forest Innovation Council (Canadian ForestService (CFS), some provinces and industry CEOs) • ever more inclusive forums leading to FPInnovations as an industry innovation hub (CFS, some provinces, industry, Forest Products Association of Canada, NSERC)	• team for process design (IMP) • community of practice to equip staff to use IMP • team for information system to support IMP
Conversations	Resolving by retooling: • on-going 2008-2011	Inquiring by restructuring and reframing: • 2003 and continuing (FPInnovations & Canadian Wood Fibre Centre as a start)	Inquiring by reframing: • 2005-2008 pilot • 2008 & continuing
Questioning principles	• integrating fragmented system	• questioning traditional approach => overcoming fragmented research system was	• research → science-based policy driven and consequent implications
New technologies	• automated inspection of authenticated POS bills	• FP Innovations around which technologies are created (e.g. for industry and for collaborative research)	• technology (IMP) • people (LOPcp) • information (ProMis)
Bricolage	• pilot project before implementation	• gradual consolidation of the fragmented research system • new products and processes along the way	• pilot project before implementation • 12 new industry pilots • Canada-US high-level press conference
Social learning	• ↓ inspection time • ↓ unfair competition • ↑ revenue recovery	• greener sector, focused on innovation and sustainability and outwards looking • new products • new bio-technology centre (Thunder Bay)	• new relationships (internal and external) • new capabilities

The project (2008-2011) created a number of public spaces for discussion and conversations among partners: one involving RQ people (200 in the core team with a variety of expertise, plus 200 others) as well as others, including IBM Canada, five associations of restaurant owners, technology installers, and a developer/manufacturer of sales recording systems. Management of the project was carried out in partnership with industry, and involved close collaboration with restaurant owners, and even some form of co-management of the project. This meant that on-going conversations took place throughout the project.

Questioning

The project amounted to finding a way of integrating what had been a fragmented and disjointed system so as to make fiscal monitoring and revenue collection more effective. Automation allowed inspection of authenticated point-of-sale bills, as well as an automatic connection to RQ's central database.

The key innovation was a sales recording module (SRM) that interconnected a restaurant's point-of-sale system, the receipt printer, the cash register, and a hand-held computer (to automate the inspection process). Each bill produced with an SRM shows the necessary information, and the SRM connects with RQ's central database.

Bricolage

A several-month long pilot project was part of the process to enable prototyping, and to ensure careful attention to small details. As a result, adjustments could be made along the way before final implementation.

For RQ, the cost of inspection decreased from $4,400 to $196 (a reduction of 96 percent). An inspection that used to take 70 hours now takes only three. Inspection files are more complete and accurate, and the reform has been well received by the associations of restaurant owners and others. More generally, Revenue Québec can now uncover fraud more easily, determine which restaurants should be prioritized for inspections and audits, and its audits can be based on more reliable books of accounts.

Canadian Forest Industry[1]

Conversations

The forestry sector in Canada is important domestically (1.9 percent of GDP, and the mainstay of the economies of 200 resource-based communities), and internationally (second largest exporter of primary forest products in the world). Globally, the sector has been changing in recent years – including building on *innovation,* and not just research *per se* (with a trend towards partnerships and integration).

By 2003, all key players in Canada had begun to recognize that a major forest industry transformation was under way, and had started to look at how research at the national level was perhaps not enabling/supporting that transformation.[2]

The first public space – the Canadian Forest Innovation Council (CFIC), made up of senior executives from federal and provincial governments and industry CEO's – was set up to "develop mechanisms to consolidate the [Forest Industry] innovation system" (CCFM Innovation Working Group 2008: 6).

The Canadian Forest Service (CFS) (staff of 750) was the logical entity to lead the discussions among the key players, but it was ill equipped to do so.[3] Innovation in the form of restructuring and reframing was required for the forest industry *in the large,* and *in the small* (i.e., in the Canadian Forest Service itself). The two innovation processes are presented separately in what follows.

---

[1] Much of what follows is based on unpublished material prepared for the IPAC Innovation Awards competition that was very kindly provided by the Canadian Forest Service (CFS).

[2] In Canada, R&D (equally funded by governments and industry) is largely divided between downstream (focused on manufacturing in three industrial research institutes) and upstream (focused on forest sustainability taking place in the Canadian Forest Service as well as in-house capacity in some provinces) – universities covered the full spectrum.

[3] It was a highly decentralized organization entirely focused on science. Well-viewed by clients for science excellence and focus on the environment, its strategic and operating priorities, however, were unknown to provincial governments and to the industry.

a) Forest industry in the large

Conversations continued with respect to industry in the large

The CFIC was the beginning of on-going conversations among the key players[4] as a means of innovating by inquiring.

Questioning

In considering how best to proceed two crucial challenges were identified for the sector: (i) fragmentation among the research institutions (i.e., organizational structure and management) and (ii) lack of 'agreed to' strategic innovation goals for the sector (i.e., products and technology). Key proposals were put forward to deal with both challenges by creating *FP Innovations* and the *Canadian Wood Fibre Centre*. FP Innovations began as the consolidation of three industrial research institutes, and evolved from there; the Canadian Wood Fibre Centre (created and housed as a virtual entity in CFS, working in partnership with FP Innovations) represented a collaboration to pursue an agreed upon avenue of innovation.

These actions were meant to help underpin an industry shift from a traditional approach (traditional products and markets, with little explicit regard for sustainability) to one that was more resilient and competitive (i.e., one that included higher-value uses, innovative processes as well as new markets, and showed real sensitivity to resource sustainability). In effect, this was the start of building *an innovation system for the industry as a whole*.

New technologies emerged over the years that followed, as the two proposals were implemented. An innovation/research hub for the sector evolved from FP Innovations (now one of the world's largest not-for-profit forest research centres).[5] This has spawned collaborations that include the National Forest Sector Transformation Strategy (involving the work of the Forest

---

[4] CFIC was later disbanded and its mandate taken over by the Board of Directors of FP Innovations.

[5] Involving the industry, governments, universities and suppliers, and a special relationship with FPAC.

Products Association of Canada (FPAC), Natural Resources Canada (of which CFS is a part), and FP Innovations) as well as the National Research Advisory Committee that guides collaborative research.

Bricolage

Building this innovation system took time, and involved prototyping and mindfulness: the gradual consolidation of the fragmented research system (i.e., the evolution of FP Innovations as the industry's innovation hub)[6] and the emergence of new products and processes along the way (e.g., comprehensive information for the construction industry about an engineered wood product (2010)).

The sector is transforming, and has become greener. The result can be seen in new products (e.g., the world's first nano crystalline cellulose production plant established by FP Innovations with Domtar (2011)) and new facilities (e.g., the biotechnology centre created by them in Thunder Bay (2012)) as well as the first comprehensive cooperation agreement to provide development support for native-owned forest companies (2012).

b) The Canadian Forest Service *per se*

CFS, as a significant player building an inquiring system for the industry, had to transform as well. Crucially, the then ADM of CFS (Brian Emmett) gave permission to senior managers at CFS to explore and take risks. As one of us was told, he said, in effect, "I don't know where we must go, but I know we must go somewhere."

Conversations continued about the CFS in the small

The focus initially was the management of R&D using a partnership with a global leader in R&D management (the consulting firm Arthur D. Little), but it soon became clear that CFS's staff needed to learn to work as part of what would have to become a 'learning organization.'

---

[6] One that has recently been extended to include academia with new aligned research networks embedded in FP Innovations.

New public discussion spaces were built as the work was carried out in the form of: (i) a cross-disciplinary team for embedding innovation in its business process; (ii) a community of practice (of 150 people in 6 regional centres)[7] to help equip staff to work in this kind of environment with this kind of business process; and (iii) another cross-disciplinary team to create the necessary information system to support that business process.

Questioning

In effect, CFS had to build its own inquiring system at its core – reframing so that it could change in several ways: change from a *research organization* to a *science-based policy organization*; from a regionally-based organization to a national one; from capacity to demand driven; from a knowledge creator to a creator and synthesizer of knowledge; and from an honest broker to an opinion-provider.

Bricolage

The process began with a pilot project (2005-2008) to determine just what innovation CFS needed, and it led to a three-pronged approach, with new mutually-reinforcing technologies being built on CFS's key comparative assets: (i) an Innovation Management Process (IMP), (ii) the equipping of people by establishing and using a community of practice (LOPcp), and (iii) a planning and information management system (ProMis) to support the process.[8]

The IMP is a coordinated business management approach supported by a governance model that empowers executive management with horizontal responsibilities (that became part of their 'day job'), while respecting inherent vertical accountability. Necessary information support comes from

---

[7] The rule of thumb to ensure organizational cultural change is that at least 20 percent of staff must be fully engaged in order for the transformation to be likely to succeed. As a result, CFS used a community of practice to equip all staff to work in the new way that comprised 150 of the total of 750.

[8] One of the key lessons learned was that 'relationships-possibilities-actions' is a fundamental principle of a learning organization, and that equal time must be spent on each front for an organization to be both resilient and effective.

ProMis. The community of practice focussed on organizational culture – helping to address the challenges of working in a more collaborative and integrated way. It honed feedback, hammered out the 80/20 rule (i.e., letting go of the need to get it right the first time, and of the need to mobilize a consensus of all partners before launching an experiment).[9]

By mid-2012, twelve pilot projects had been launched under NRCan's Transformative Technology Program. And a binational forest health summit had been held with US counterparts to identify shared research priorities on which both countries could collaborate.[10]

An independent 2012 evaluation found a transformation of both position and perspective in CFS.

Discussion of the two cases

Conversations

In both cases the issue was ripe for attention.

Addressing the issue involved a number of public spaces that brought together people with different perspectives and different knowledge, information and experience, as well as a willingness to invest the time and effort to collaborate. The conversations were ongoing over a considerable period of time.

Questioning

The Resto Project is an innovation that involves *retooling* to overcome the fragmentation of the restaurant system in Québec so as to improve the effectiveness of fiscal monitoring and revenue collection.

The Forest Industry case, on the other hand, is about building inquiring systems (using *restructuring* and *reframing* to overcome system fragmentation in government-industry-

---

[9] This work 'in the small' provides an example of a 'plan-do-learn-adjust' manifestation and focus.

[10] This brought together senior level funders, users, and performers, and a joint press release was issued at the political level. (Five years before, CFS would not have had the influence or the ability to orchestrate a binational press release at such a high level.)

university innovation/research) so as to transform the industry and the governing regime charged with a key stewardship role.

Bricolage

Both cases proceeded by feeling their way. In the Resto Project, this included keeping a close link with restaurant owners as well as piloting what they had developed so as to improve it before implementation. The Forest Industry Project was more complex and needed to proceed in steps, the nature of which were not clear beforehand, and the scope of its reach increased gradually in stages. What was being built was an inquiring system.

Connectors

Both cases involved connectors – people who have not just the necessary experience and capability, but also the ability to span different worlds, and have the combination of curiosity, self-confidence, sociability, and energy to enable/engineer the links that can give rise to the necessary collaboration. Partnerships were necessary for the Resto Project's success, and they had to be engineered. It was also crucial in the Forest Industry Project both in the large and the small. In this case, it likely would not have been possible to have achieved as much without the work of key connectors (e.g., Avrim Lazar, former federal policy senior bureaucrat who became President and CEO of the FPAC in early 2002; the first ADM of CFS (Brian Emmett); and director and then director general, Mary Mes-Hartree – the 'driving force' within CFS – as one of us was told).

Mindfulness

In both cases, success depended upon attention being paid to details.

For the Resto Project, examples include the monitoring of the project itself (using committees, internal monitoring mechanisms and management indicators) as well as ensuring that the direct impact on restaurant owners was minimized (e.g., working with some associations of restaurant owners and establishing a help line for restaurant owners generally).

For the Forest Industry Project, building an industry inquiring system necessarily meant paying ongoing attention to small details by listening to the feedback from key stakeholders and others, as well as from results and outcomes. And it has been reported that transforming CFS into a learning organization success was only possible because the details of the business process and the information system to support it were sound and usable by all who needed to feed it or use it.

Lessons learned and modest general propositions

It would be foolhardy to attempt any generalizations from our limited exploration, but it would be equally unreasonable not to try to draw some lessons from what we have observed. We have chosen to couch our learning in the form of six modest general propositions (MGP) that might be regarded as propositions that would deserve to be explored further and put to a test.

How does the issue emerge and crystallize into a policy problem? How does a meaningful forum get created?

MGP 1
Some commonalities (shared concern or interest) have to exist, and/or some confluence of events has to bring them forth to allow a language community to materialize.

How are interpretative conversations kept alive?

MGP 2
Some capable connectors who knowing enough about the mega-community, and the way the government works, can make an immense amount of difference in the way the issue evolves as a policy problem.

How is the new technology (principles and ways) brought forth?

MGP 3

An innovation is more likely to materialize around a new principle (collaboration) if and when partnerships involve quite different parties, each of which is quite clear about the different resources each partner brings and/or makes available to the table.

How do the new technologies (material, organizational, intellectual) gain traction?

MGP 4

Consensus is not needed for an innovation process to gain traction. It seems as if strong commitment from 20 percent of core participants is enough to carry the movement forward.

How is the new technology implemented?

MGP 5

Social learning means trying something and learning how to improve it as one proceeds. Letting go of the need to get it right the first time has to be defended forcefully and effectively in the public sector on both the internal and the external fronts.

MGP 6

Social learning may only thrive on small wins that the organization can build on, and it would appear that an essential ingredient in generating these small wins is mindfulness.

References

Arthur, W. Brian. 2009. *The Nature of Technology*. New York, NY: Free Press.

Boisvert, Raymond D. 1998. *John Dewey – Rethinking Our Time*. Albany, NY: State University of New York Press.

Boland, Richard J. and Fred Collopy (eds.). 2004. *Managing by Design*. Stanford, CA: Stanford University Press.

Brown, Tim. 2009. *Change by Design*. New York, NY: HarperCollins.

CCFM Innovation Working Group. 2008. "Forest Sector Innovation Framework." Report prepared for the Canadian Council of Forest Ministers. www.ccfm.org/pdf/FSIF-FINAL_E.pdf [Accessed November 5, 2014].

FPInnovations. 2011-2012. "Building on our Successes." Annual report developed for FPInnovations, Pointe-Claire, QC, www.fpinnovations.ca/MediaCentre/AnnualReports/fpinnovations-2011-2012_annual_report.pdf [Accessed November 5, 2014]. See also www.fpinnovations.ca/InnovationHub/Pages/developing-an-innovation-hub.aspx and www.fpinnovations.ca/Organization/Pages/get-to-know-us-organization.aspx [Accessed November 5, 2014].

Gehry, Frank. 1999. "Commentaries" in M. Friedman (ed.). *Architecture + process: Gehry talks*. New York, NY: Rizzoli, p. 43-287.

Gerencser, Mark *et al.* 2008. *Megacommunities*. New York, NY: Palgrave Macmillan.

Hock, Dee. 1999. *Birth of the Chaordic Age*. San Francisco, CA: Berrett-Koehler.

Lester, Richard K. and Michael J. Piore. 2004. *Innovation – The Missing Dimension*. Cambridge, MA: Harvard University Press.

March, James G. 1991. "Exploration and Exploitation in Organizational Learning," *Organization Science*, 2: 71-87.

Natural Resources Canada. 2012. "A Journey of Transformation for the Canadian Forest Service," http://www.ipac.ca/documents/NaturalResourcesCanada.pdf [Accessed November 5, 2014].

Natural Resources Canada. 2012. "The CFS Transformation Story," (unpublished, (i) Presentation and (ii) Submission).

Paquet, Gilles. 2005. *The New Geo-Governance – A Baroque Approach.* Ottawa, ON: University of Ottawa Press.

Paquet, Gilles and Christopher Wilson. 2012, "Inquiring Systems," in R. Hubbard, G. Paquet, and C. Wilson. *Stewardship.* Ottawa, ON: Invenire Books, p. 31-54.

Patton, Michael Quinn. 2011. *Developmental Evaluation – Applying Complexity Concepts to Enhance Innovation and Use.* New York, NY: The Guilford Press.

Revenue Québec. 2012. *The Resto Project: Mandatory Billing in the Restaurant Sector.* Winnipeg, MB: Institute of Public Administration Canada (IPAC), www.ipac.ca/documents/RevenuQuebec.pdf [Accessed November 5, 2014].

Weick, Karl E. 2004. "Rethinking Organizational Design" in Richard J. Boland and Fred Collopy (eds.). *Managing by Design.* Stanford, CA: Stanford University Press, p. 36-53.

Weick, Karl E. and Kathleen M. Sutcliffe. 2007 (2nd ed.). *Managing the Unexpected – Resilient Performance in an Age of Uncertainty.* New York, NY: John Wiley & Sons.

| The Management Vacuum: Peril III

Ruth Hubbard and Gilles Paquet

> "A fundamental mismatch exists between today's workforce and workplace, and the institutions and policies that support and govern them."
>
> *Thomas A. Kochan*

Introduction

I n any governing arrangement there are, at times, gaps and failings that generate performance failures. Some of these gaps and failures have only minor impacts, and may be tolerated without much inconvenience. Others, however, are so damning that they put acute pressure on organizations for adjustments because of their dramatic impact on performance. One would like to believe that such pressure manages to translate in quick and effective repairs and innovations to correct the situation, but this is not the case. Rather often, the flawed arrangements that are socially costly are also personally gratifying to some individuals and groups, who draw benefit from such circumstances, and therefore oppose any repairs that would deprive them of what they regard as their well-deserved entitlements in terms of power or perks.

In a recent book (Hubbard and Paquet 2014a), we have documented serious inadequacies in the performance of some senior executives in the Canadian federal public service. We have shown, as a result of exchanges with about 100 bright and engaged executives, that these inadequacies may be ascribed in good part to some organizational/ institutional gaps, and to some cognitive/behavioural deficiencies (*Ibid.*: 127) that call for repairs at the structural and competencies levels.

In both cases, what is called for is *innovation*:

(a) in order to refocus the federal public household on high performance, and to ensure a maintenance of this focus on eliminating waste as part of daily life; and,

(b) in order to ensure a better match between the competencies required to perform ever more complex jobs, and the capacities of the workforce charged with those tasks.

Such innovations are bound to dramatically question and transform the standard routines in good currency in the Canadian federal services, and therefore to disserve those who have been building their power and authority on the existing arrangements.

In the rest of the chapter, we, first, make a succinct case for precise suggestions about the sort of innovation that is called for, and about how they could be implemented:

- *at the structural level*, the creation of external boards of management for departments and agencies; and,
- *at the competencies level*, a new human resources management regime that gives an immensely more important role to a competencies approach.

Second, in each case we spell out what these innovations would do, and how they would work. Finally, we remind the reader of the reasons why these very simple suggestions have not been implemented already but have been (and are still) vociferously opposed, and we suggest a promising way to kick-start the process that might lead to their being widely adopted in the Canadian federal public service.

Driving out part of the fake in public administration

There are various ways in which the Canadian federal public household may be said to be less than optimally governed. But two specific interfaces are particularly problematic: first, the interface between the public household and the citizenry it is meant to serve, on the demand side so to speak; and second, the interface between the public household as a quasi-firm and its workforce, on the supply side.

The public household/citizenry interface

On the first front, all sorts of general forces have dramatically modified the interface between the public household and the citizenry over the past 60 years. One such force is a broad increase in the scope of government services provided to the citizenry with the advent of the welfare state – with a consequent significant growth in the size of the public household, and in the complexity of its operations. In a society that has become more variegated, and where individuals and groups have become capable of expressing their preferences more and more robustly, the challenge of meeting these diverse expectations has also become more daunting.

Yet as the public household grew, it also became more and more inward looking and self-centred. The organizational challenge of running such a multi-faceted enterprise absorbed more and more energy, and the temptation to adjust the *modus operandi* to make the task less awkward and less daunting has triggered the development of more mechanisms of centralization and homogenization of services, and a certain desensitization *vis-à-vis* the idiosyncrasies of the different segments of the population. Effectiveness in reaching the citizen gave way to standardization and ways of operation that were more convenient for bureaucrats. This created a cleavage between the bureaucracy and the citizenry, and a lesser concern for doing the right thing (effectiveness) as opposed to a greater concern for doing the thing right (efficiency) – i.e., according to rules likely to be audited.

To this broad and sweeping bureaucratization wave in Canada was added a particular ideological bent that materialized, from the 1960s on (as a result of the *zeitgeist* of the time), the plague of minority governments, a growth of activism on the union front, and a particular idealistic/romantic 'progressive' virus that took hold of a significant portion of the elected officials, the media and the intelligentsia.

This maelstrom materialized in the form of a series of determining turns of events: (a) the pursuit of a so-called 'model employer' philosophy by the Canadian federal government (with all sorts of concerns extraneous to performance like diversity, equality and the like, overriding completely concerns for effectiveness); and (b) a particularly weak and bizarre reaction by government to illegal strike action by postal workers, by granting the right to unionize and strike to nearly all federal employees. These developments have shifted the focus of the public household even further away from concerns about effectiveness, performance and productivity, toward doing the thing right (process, inward concerns about labour peace, and the like).

As these forces created a greater and greater disconnect between the operations of the public household and its performance, this schism was rationalized as responding to the fundamental discontinuity between the sorts of 'higher' concerns that the public household has to deal with, and the usual concerns of interest in the private sector, and the assertion that those higher concerns called for a totally different way of governing in which performance, effectiveness and the like are only part of a much larger equation.

This allowed the insertion of an immense *fuzz factor* in the administration of the public household, as compared with what was happening elsewhere. All sorts of considerations were said to be of such import that they could justify a generalized lack of concern with effectiveness and performance in the name of those other considerations. Public administration became absorbed with processes, and more and more immunized from concerns about management and performance.

Bureaucratic imperatives became dominant, and an increase in sophistry helped to rationalize whatever aberration or *bizarrerie* needed to be rationalized. Indeed, among the public household clergy, nothing appeared to be more rational than a rationalization. This was to underpin a philosophy of 'anything goes' in the name of a difference of kind between the public and the private sectors. And to those who might object that this was hardly the way to run a business, the answer was simply that government is not anything like business. What ensued has been a centralized system of control that claims to run the public household top-down, with formal mechanisms that allow so much whimsicality down the hierarchy that Kafkaesque results ensued (Hubbard and Paquet 2010).

For a while, such *obiter dictu* appeared to carry the day. It took a disastrous performance of major proportions to open the door to the revolution of public choice, and to the temptation to initiate new public management processes. But by that time, the public administration ideology had sufficiently crystallized that the public administration tribe (academics and practitioners) could enter the battle with the new barbarians outside the gate (who claimed that much in the public household could share management tools with the private sector) well-armed.

It became an epic battle between an inspired 'progressive' public administration class and a 'common-sense' public management posse. That battle has been fought and won quite differently depending on which battlefield is scrutinized. In the public administration literature, victory has been declared *ab ovo* by a clergy that has been satisfied with denouncing the barbarians who do not understand the quintessence of public administration. Elsewhere, the management vacuum of traditional public administration has been recognized, but corporate interests in the public household – quite comfortable with the prevailing fuzz – have understandably resisted. No one has committed hara-kiri, some superficial management improvements have been clumsily added on, but little has been done to eliminate the penumbra and the fake that it makes possible.

The public household/workforce interface

On the second front, there is the interface between the public household and its workforce. It has been allowed to slump into a state that generates great inefficiency, not only (a) as a result of the complete disconnect between the organization and performance imperatives, because of the lack of pressure to perform, but also (b) as a result of the disenfranchising of performance (and management) as not being central to the concerns of the public household. The focus on 'model employer' was allowed to run awry, allowing the human resources function to become dysfunctional. Instead of designing a human resources (HR) function to achieve performance, the HR function was perverted into focusing on catering to the comfort of the workforce as an objective unto itself.

This has entailed a relaxation of the HR regime to the point of allowing (except in certain areas regulated by external bodies) the real matching of the capacities of the human resources and the complexities of the job to become somewhat subsidiary in the staffing function. This is more obvious as one climbs the hierarchical ladder, since the job requirements tend to become fuzzier there, leaving a greater margin of maneuverability for whims. The reasons for the necessary looseness of the linkage between the capabilities of the human resources and the complexities of the job (especially at the upper end of the HR scale) – it is argued – are the difficulties of gauging these features. More realistically, it can be argued that any effort to develop and finesse a meaningful way to gauge these features has been avoided because of the new constraints they would entail for executives in the running of the public household.

No one would deny that these features are difficult to define in useful and reliable ways. But in some agencies, like the Canada Revenue Agency, it has proved both a possible and a tractable task. As for the corporatist opposition to such gauging (again, outside the realm of externally regulated competencies) in the name of higher-order ethereal and ineffable qualities being necessary to dispatch the sort of *different in kind* tasks in the public household: it may be hogwash, but it has become a foundational myth in the public administration tribe, and has been carefully sustained over time, in academe and elsewhere, with sponsored studies feeding on financial support from the federal bureaucracy itself (Kernaghan 2007).

This mental prison has been powerful enough to ensure that concern about the matching of capacities with the complexities of the task has been kept at bay. It is seen as not relevant to public household work, especially at the senior levels. The disinterest in finding ways to improve this matching has resulted in poor matching – a problem exacerbated by the carousel of senior executives among the various departments since Pierre Trudeau's days – and the cost of this mismatch, while it has not yet been satisfactorily quantified, can only be conjectured to be enormous.

Both flawed interfaces re-enforce each other

Both these flawed interfaces in the Canadian federal public household are consequential, and they re-enforce each other. Less concern about performance breeds laxity in matching capacities and the complexities of the tasks, and poor matching can only breed ineffectiveness, poor performance, and waste.

It is our view that innovation on both fronts *at the same time* could dramatically transform the effectiveness and performance of the public household. There are obviously many ways in which improvements might be achieved on both fronts. But there is much merit, in a zone of waste that for a long time has neglected to deal with precise management discussions about mechanisms to achieve better focus on performance and matching, in proceeding not with general wishful statements, but with very precise proposals so as to be able to explain clearly what might be done and how it would work.

The tool we propose on the first front is the creation of *boards of management for all departments and agencies* in the Canadian federal government unless, for important reasons, it can be claimed to be totally unsuitable. These boards would focus explicitly on performance, not in complete ignorance of the overall mission of the unit, but as a *subsidiary board* charged with performance within the constraints defined by the policy framework and the senior board, and charged with continuous feedback with the senior board (the whole-of-government board) so as to ensure that there is no disconnect between the policy level and the management level, and that mutual social learning ensues.

The tool we propose on the second front is *a competencies approach* to the HR regime, one that would ensure the matching of capacities and the complexities of the tasks. It is not a matter of mechanically imposing a particular scheme, but of using a generic framework and vocabulary to develop a made-in-Canada framework that would fit our particular circumstances and traditions.

In both cases, there will be opposition to these proposals. Some will claim it impossible to implement; others will argue that it would prevent public sector executives from doing their jobs. We argue that there is a need to set up an inquiring system, not only to find the best fit on both the structural and competencies fronts (given the Canadian circumstances), but also to enable the appropriate social learning and the requisite time to learn and adapt well when changeovers are required.

We suggest that these innovations be developed experimentally first in half a dozen departments or agencies, and that once the prototypes have been played with sufficiently to finesse them and have proven them resilient but also capable of making the system antifragile (i.e., capable of becoming stronger as the challenges they meet are more robust), they be generalized to all department and agencies where it is suitable (Taleb 2012). This might be accomplished fully within one decade. The main purpose of this transition period is to have ample time to *drive out the fake* – not only to finesse the right organizational instruments that are needed in particular circumstances, but also to allow mental prisons to be unlocked, and the cosmologies to adapt, so that the mental blockages that have played such a destructive role in preventing these innovations to take hold up to now, can be neutralized and attenuated, if not made to disappear.

Boards of management

This is not a new idea, but one whose time has come, albeit in a somewhat different form from what has been proposed by the likes of Peter Aucoin.

Concern about the under-performance of the traditional departments and agencies of the Canadian federal government (but elsewhere as well) was strongly felt in the 1970s and 1980s but was systematically underplayed by the choirmasters of the public administration enterprise in Canada. Only the financial crisis of the early 1990s – that forced the program review exercise onto the government's agenda – managed to bring forth real concern about increasing service delivery efficiency. It materialized in the form of the 1995 framework for alternative service delivery (Canada 1995).

The key word was *efficiency*. This framework was not really directed at making government more *effective* (i.e., doing the right thing) but at making it more *efficient* (i.e., doing the thing right). This led to a tendency to tinker with the technology of the service delivery segment at the tail end of the policy funnel – going from policy formation, program design, to the mechanisms for service delivery – in quasi-complete isolation of what was happening upstream, and, therefore, without the crucially important feedback loop with the policy formation stage of the policy funnel. This echoed the view of some academics like Aucoin, who mistakenly argued that the policy funnel can be tightly segmented into disconnected pieces without important malefits ensuing (Aucoin 1995, 1996).

This sort of deeply flawed thinking was based on a strong version of three ill-founded assumptions:

(a) the separability of policy formation, program design, and delivery mechanism;

(b) the sacredness of accountability to the minister, Westminster-style; and,

(c) the presumption that detailed contracts would suffice to ensure that the policies intended by ministers and senior officials are carried out down the policy funnel most effectively.

Aucoin (first period in the 1990s) held these assumptions dear, and he was wrong. Separability is toxic because it stunts social learning; and ministerial accountability, conceived for a Big G world, has become attenuated in a small-g world (where power, resources and information are widely distributed in many hands). In a small-g world, detailed contracts do not suffice to link the various segments of the policy funnel – social learning loops are required. The 'cartoonesque' characterization based on the above assumptions may explain why the alternative service delivery (ASD) initiatives built on it failed. One cannot tinker separately with service delivery without some serious rethinking of all the other segments of the whole policy funnel (Paquet 1997).

To make it more likely for departments/agencies (a) to put a greater focus on management and service to the citizenry in an *effectiveness-cum-efficiency mode,* as well as (b) to maintain a strong traditionally higher-order 'partnering' with government policy work upstream, effective arrangements need to be found: an appropriate structure providing both freedom and flexibility, while accepting the constraint of effective central oversight and accountability for a performance that is mission-driven.

An effective external but embedded board of management must remain a subsidiary board, and this can be accomplished if the deputy head is always a member of that board, and ensures continuous liaison between the whole-of-government board and the board of management of the department/agency – a liaison that works both ways by providing and receiving feedback at both ends.

Aucoin (second period in the late 2000s) may have *appeared* to have evolved toward a position calling for continuous necessary feedback loops between segments (Aucoin 2007), and Heintzman and Juillet (2012) may also have *appeared* to concur and to adopt a softer position than Aucoin (first period) if only by not addressing the issue head-on. In fact, neither paper is entirely clear about the extent to which the authors adhere strongly or loosely to the basic assumption of absolute separability among the different segments of the policy funnel. However, to the extent that they all seem to embrace separability of an extreme sort *upstream* – between politicians and senior bureaucrats, for instance – to the point of denouncing a culture of "promiscuity"[1] where less paranoid observers would only see effective collaboration, they must be suspected of still harbouring the same ill-inspired devotion to absolute separability, and to an anti-promiscuity bias, all the way along the downstream segments of the policy funnel.

Most certainly the tone of the last paper by Peter Aucoin, (before he passed away) would still appear to embrace somewhat incoherently (Aucoin 2012):[2]

(a) a tightly segmented view of how the different portions of the policy funnel should interface (and, with it, a phobia of promiscuity);

(b) an ultimate deference to the integrated and hierarchical Westminster system as a sacred cow; and,

(c) a presumption that one can define detailed contracts among the segments of the policy funnel, to ensure that the policies intended by the senior board and senior officials are carried out down the policy funnel most effectively.

This would suggest that *Aucoin would not support our sort of board of management*: one that does not presume that such detailed contracts can be drawn up, and one that therefore calls for active collaboration among segments of the policy funnel, and therefore some promiscuity in order to ensure synoptic social learning, even though *en dernière instance*, the political authority would prevail. Our sort of board of management is briefly described below.

[1] This is the very strong word used and re-used uncritically by Aucoin but also by Heintzman (2014).

[2] These speculative reflections about what academic disputations might support are of minimal interest, since, in recent times, Canada has experimented *in real time and in real life* with an initiative that has already been implemented successfully at the Canada Revenue Agency – one that has met with great success, and has led to CRA also initiating a competencies approach to its HR regime as a fringe benefit (Hubbard and Paquet 2014a).

What these boards of management would do

In many countries, the experience with boards of management has been initiated with the creation of agencies as an alternative for the traditional departments to escape many of the constraints inherited from department-centred structures that are hierarchical, centrally-controlled organizations, slow to adapt to changing conditions, and inadequately responsive to the interests they serve (Schick 2002).

Unlike Aucoin, Schick appears to see boards of management as focusing on performance and management, but subject to the broad direction of the whole-of-government board, and committed to functional integration by working hard at striking a balance, at the operational level, between coordination and subordination, cooperation and conflict.

In the case of the boards of management that we propose, this would entail that they would take responsibility for finance, human resources, procurement, assets management, and information technology, and the like. The two boards would work in tandem, with as much autonomy as possible granted to the subsidiary board, but with an explicit recognition that, depending on the nature of the work involved, more or less of the above mentioned activities might be abandoned – more or less fully – to the subsidiary board.

The Canada Revenue Agency (CRA) provides an example. Its mission is to "… administer tax, benefit, and related programs and to ensure compliance on behalf of governments across Canada …" (CRA 2011: 3). It assesses, collects, and administers hundreds of billions of dollars in tax revenue every year, including directly delivering billions in benefits and tax credits. To do this, in 2012-13, it had the equivalent of about 40,000 people full time, and a budget of over $4.25 billion.

For our purposes, CRA activities can be thought of as involving three levels of players: 1) the whole of government (the 'big' management board, Treasury Board and its supporting secretariat), the responsible minister (the Minister of Revenue), and the Governor-in Council); 2) a subsidiary board of management in order to keep a clear focus on performance;

and, 3) the Agency itself, headed by its commissioner (the most senior bureaucrat).

A subsidiary board of management was established to oversee the CRA's organization and administration. The 15-person majority external (including the chair) board, sits between the responsible minister and the agency. The accountability of the most-senior bureaucrat (the commissioner) for day-to-day management rests with the board and its four committees: audit; governance; human resources; and resources (e.g., financial).

The commissioner is *de facto* a member of the board, and is responsible for the Agency's management, the supervision of its employees, and the implementation of its policies and budgets. The Agency's decision-making body (the Agency Management Committee (AMC) chaired by the commissioner) is supported, in turn, by six sub-committees that deal with: strategic direction; resource and investment management; human resources; strategic operations; and tactical operations, including making recommendations on matters to be decided by AMC. The sixth subcommittee – Management Audit and Evaluation – (responsible for oversight of internal audits and program evaluations) reports to the Board's Audit Committee rather than to AMC.

How these boards of management would work

As hinted at above, the working arrangements between the two boards might be modulated (with a different division of labour, and a greater or lower degree of full autonomy for the junior board) depending on the nature of the unit's mission. But whatever arrangements might be deemed workable, some crucial imperatives would prevail.

Depending on the relative importance of policy work in the daily activities of the unit, more or less of the operational activities may be ceded to the subsidiary board with more or less important liens being imposed as constraints. To fix ideas, one might partition the units into three batches (α: those where all the activities mentioned above are ceded completely to the subsidiary board; β: those where only some of the activities with diverse liens are ceded; γ: those where a minimal set of activities – regarded as the *minimum minimorum* required for the system to function – are ceded) according to circumstances and the relative omnipresence (or not) of policy concerns or not in the operations of the unit.

Overriding all these idiosyncrasies, it should be understood that (a) the proposed principles of operation of the board of management for the management of the unit would be scrutinized by the senior board, and subject to discussion and negotiations, and ultimately to a directive of the senior board establishing what will need to prevail in the final analysis; and (b) a continuous process of exchange of information between the two boards would ensure effective social learning.

Finally, any such refurbished agency/department may remain somewhat constrained by other authorities within the overall governing apparatus – provincial constraints being respected, wide-ranging authority of commissioners of one sort or another, etc.

Again, the CRA provides a concrete example. The government as a whole uses three main levers to situate and control the CRA. They deal with: (a) management overall; (b) the grey zone between management and policy, as well as matters materially affecting public finance; and (c) the appointment of members of the CRA Board of Management. The CRA Board maintains an overall degree of control over CRA management (e.g., approval of its corporate business plan and negotiating mandates with unions), including requiring a degree of consistency in presentation of material with respect to public finances (e.g., approval of annual resource requests, and performance results set out in terms of strategic outcomes). It may also (via the responsible minister) issue a written directive to that board on any matter within the board's authority that affects public policy, or could materially affect public finances. It may also (via the responsible minister) receive advice on management matters from that board.

The oversight framework enables the CRA Board to assess performance with respect to the five required areas of oversight (organization, administration, resources, services, and personnel) (CRA 2013-14). The framework includes expectations for each area, assessment criteria, information considered in arriving at a rating, and the ratings themselves of strong, acceptable, opportunity for improvement, or unacceptable (requiring immediate attention).

A list of competencies has been developed for the CRA Board Chair (e.g., communications and public relations, corporate governance, strategic outlook and alignment) and individual directors (e.g., collegiality and mature confidence, ethics, integrity and accountability, informed and sound judgement) as well as the overall needs of that board (e.g., change management, complex multi-dimensional client service, human resources and labour negotiations) (CRA 2012-13).

Social learning of all key players is enabled in a number of ways: (a) from the formal reporting that is required by the government, along with any written directives to the CRA Board or advice from it – this formal reporting feeds into the senior management board and is necessarily potentially affected by it, including by any written directives from the responsible minister and any advice from the Board to that minister; (b) by the use of the CRA Board's performance assessment that 'informs' the objectives in the Commissioner's Performance Agreement as well as the Board and its committees' work plans (CRA 2011); (c) by the on-going activities of internal audit and program evaluation, and via the results of the CRA Board's overview of risk and change management.

Competencies approach to staffing

This second idea is not new either. It would appear quite commonsensical to select personnel by matching the capabilities of the candidates as much as possible with the competencies needed to perform the task well. However, to the extent that performance has not been a central concern, and that the very notion of competencies has been made extraordinarily evasive by allowing the missions of the public household to become more ethereal, the capabilities evoked as central for success in public household work have been tended to become more ethereal also, so this interface has become immensely mushy.

In fact, especially at the senior executive levels, the reliance on a solid concern for competencies has become displaced by all sorts of intangible and whimsical qualities or reference points that have been evoked as crucial requirements for the job. No persuasive rationale has been provided for these evanescent and impressionistic appreciations, nor any effort made to generate or provide reliable indicators for such things, nor any initiative launched to confirm that such elusive guideposts ensured the selection of candidates who have proved successful in the position.

All this staffing work has continued unquestioned even though it was conducted in rather whimsical ways (outside of jobs where externally run professional bodies could provide detailed specifications for competencies) because of a veneer of formal processes that may have satisfied the bureaucratic mind that it could assure that good performance would follow appointments made in this manner, but most certainly did not satisfy anyone else.

Anyone scrutinizing the selection process in the public household quickly realizes that while it may be said to be relatively reliable at the lowest and most routinized jobs level (where the sheer number of candidates to be processed and the potentialities for appeal have forced a certain rationalization onto the process, and a certain demonstrability of efficacy and fairness), and in the case of professionally and technically well-defined jobs (where external standards are well established), it is not the case in the higher echelons of the public household. At these higher echelons, the criteria invoked are ever more evasive, the gauging immensely more subjective, and the marksmanship a matter never scrutinized.

The propensity for the public administration academic literature to be content to operate at such stratospheric 'cloudish' levels, and not to allow itself to slump down much to the level of the mechanics of public household management, has meant that the degree of evasiveness in good currency has not been truly scrutinized and denounced as a source of ineffectiveness in the public service. Rather, academics have produced some hagiographic literature designed to comfort senior executives of the public sector in their view that their work is incommensurable with the work done in the other sectors, and that the quasi-ecclesiastical ways in which they are selected is commensurate with their ineffable missionary tasks. Both academics and practitioners have seemingly come to agree that it would be almost *un crime de lèse-majesté* to probe too deeply into those processes.

The result has been the perpetuation of haphazard processes of selection that remained immunized against any serious effort to gauge their effectiveness. Yet any observer of the bureaucratic scene has been quite aware of the whimsicality of the processes and of the toxicity of the results. However, the criminal neglect of performance in the governance of the public household, and the equally criminal celebration of the opacity of the staffing process at the senior level in the public household has continued to prevail.

Our idea of a competencies approach follows.

What a competencies approach would entail

Hubbard and Paquet (2014b) has presented a Jaques-inspired description of the competencies approach (Jaques 2002).

The concern with competencies emerges from a central interest in matching the capabilities of officials with the complexity (cognitive and otherwise) of the tasks with which they are likely to be confronted. This requires an accurate appreciation of the complexity of the specific tasks to be handled, and a very effective way to gauge the capabilities of humans supposedly charged with these responsibilities. Why? Because the fuzzier the appreciation of the complexity of the task and of the competencies required, and the 'fudgier' the appreciation of the capabilities of the candidate, the more inadequate the decision about selecting a person for the job is likely to be.

The notion of competency is undoubtedly very complex. It is based on a mix of qualifications and capabilities for complex work, skills pertaining to specialized areas, commitment, and behavioural requirements to do work of quality in the face of tasks of various complexities. It is a world where quality is a somewhat imprecise word connoting a degree of expertise, savoir-faire, savoir-être, and a professional commitment to meet high standards. In that sense, the notion of competency is quite different from the notions of savoirs or knowledge which are only some necessary components of capabilities, but most certainly not sufficient components to ensure competency to deliver the sort of high quality services senior federal executives are meant to provide.

The first component of the competencies problematique is the development of some appreciation of the degree of complexity of the task. This appreciation leads to identifying various strata or levels of complexity that entail a shorter or longer time horizon (from hours to days to decades) to dispatch the work well. Six levels are used by Jaques, and are listed for illustration purposes: activities requiring concrete specified output, cumulative and corrective approaches, serial approaches, parallel processing, conceptual abstract data, and conceptual abstract information.

The second component is an appreciation of the information or mental processing capabilities of humans. These information processing capabilities can obviously be applied to problems of growing complexity dealing with tangible entities, collections of tangible entities, intangible entities, categories of intangible entities, categories of categories, and principles.

The third component is the recognition that the applicable capabilities of humans depend on many things and not only on current potential capabilities as measured by the sophistication of the mental information processing a person is capable of using. In the language of Jaques,

$$AC = f\ CPC \bullet K/S \bullet C \bullet RB$$

where	AC	=	applicable capability
	CPC	=	current potential capability measured by the sophistication of mental processing
	K/S	=	skilled knowledge for the particular problem
	C	=	commitment for the particular problem area
	RB	=	ability or inability to carry out the behaviours required by society.

The fourth component is the *maturation process of potential cognitive capabilities* as the individual ages. This is the result of an extrapolation based on extensive observations by Jaques and consorts, and it has led to the inference that, as an individual grows in age, his/her potential capability increases and, therefore, his/her capabilities to tackle more complex issues also increase.

The CRA example provides a good demonstration of the competencies approach to staffing. It has developed a list of 17 (behavioural) core competencies and 34 technical competencies (i.e., necessary knowledge and skills) (CRA 2012). Included are a number of competencies that involve the cognitive capability to handle task complexity, as well as the affinity for and commitment to a specific job (e.g., developing or leading others) (*Ibid.*). A job competency profile has been created for each job (no small task – over 1,200, covering more than 40,000 employees) and staffing decisions are based on assessments of individual competencies against those profiles (CRA 2011: 15-16). Performance management includes a discussion of an employee's competencies, and how they contribute to personal accountabilities and business objectives, while competencies also feed into learning plans that are developed to address gaps (*Ibid.*: 16). The catalogue of competencies is updated from time to time to reflect what is needed.

How a competencies approach would work

In the case of detected misfits, or less than fully satisfactory individual performance, capability gaps would have to be repaired. At all levels, this would mean using conversations/ discussions between an individual and her/his manager that are both formal (i.e., systematic performance management) and informal (e.g., personal effectiveness appraisal), as well as providing any necessary development/training, coaching, etc., to fill gaps.

This would involve a number of stages, with a reasonable/appropriate degree of investment in each. The stages would involve:

- routine informal and systematic formal performance conversations/discussions that provide feedback and set timelines for action to improve performance;
- provision of reasonable mentoring, coaching, development, or training as needed (including the possibility, under some circumstances, of job shifts to achieve better alignment);
- the use of increasingly-severe mechanisms to signal the continued presence of unacceptable gaps that constrain individual performance (e.g., withholding scheduled pay increments, demotion); and,
- the termination of employment after other reasonable avenues of repair have failed.

Given the fact that both tasks and individuals evolve, there is a need for a constant monitoring of the competencies/capabilities interface, and for tinkering with both in order to ensure goodness of fit.

The tasks are tractable, and the resistance can be overcome, so an experiment is warranted

Any initiative of such magnitude at the higher level of the Canadian public service is bound to run into a number of stumbling blocks – the most important ones being anchored in the structure and culture of the federal public service that has over time generated bad habits and rigidities of all sorts. It is unreasonable to anticipate that this sort of situation will not generate opposition from those whose habits and gratifications are challenged.

Resistance

Throughout the text, we have referred in passing to some of these mental prisons and other potential blockages that needed to be overcome. They may be summarized in the form of propensities:

a) to give dominant priority to the policy formation end of the policy funnel to the detriment of management;

b) to centralize unduly in order to gain control of the process, and to presume that whatever is ordained at the higher level will be carried out down the chain of command – much of the recent literature has shown how ineffective this Big G form of governance is, both because of cognitive limitations at the top, and behavioural, organizational and institutional obstacles down the implementation road;

c) to grant clergy-like status to senior executives in the Canadian public household, and to immunize them from the sorts of constraints imposed on others;

d) to anthropomorphize much of public administration and thereby be led to ignore important systemic dimensions that have an impact on the capacity to transform the governance of the public household – such systemic dimensions not only prevent individuals from taking reasonable decisions, but also extinguish innovative capabilities altogether;

e) to allow the public household to fall into pneumopathological states – the state of those who are morally insane, living as it where in a fantasy world of self-righteousness, and in denial *vis-à-vis* the toxicity of the arrangements in place – this leads to systematically indulging plausible deniability and uncritically accepting surreal schemes;

f) to restrict debates about reform to general principles, instead of recognizing that the devil is in the details, and carrying out precise experiments that can demonstrate whether an initiative is indeed or is not a good answer to the present challenges.[3]

---

[3] It is not very useful for navigation to be satisfied with recommendations that the public service should be focusing on the long term, that it should not be fearful of failure, that there should be more "independent, evidence-based decision-making" (whatever this may mean), and that the Canada School of Public Service should transform from an innocuous and not very useful institution to become a more daring and controversial think-tank. Fortunately, to this somewhat ethereal wish list, David McLaughlin has added one useful suggestion: "stop the churn of deputy ministers turnover" – a practical suggestion that would help much in ensuring that the capacities of the senior executives would better match the complexities of the task (McLaughlin 2014).

We have documented all of these over the last few years (Hubbard and Paquet 2010, 2014a, b; Paquet 2014). Not taking these factors into account will only increase the risk that the innovative initiatives will be successfully torpedoed.

While it is natural for the bureaucracy to protect its corporatist interests, it is criminal negligence to allow such pressure to remain unchecked when it threatens to sabotage the effectiveness of the public household. So it is essential that some critical thinking kick in, and that the initiative be accompanied by an explicit discussion of these toxic propensities, in order to ensure that they are tamed to the extent that they cannot prevent the implementation of necessary reforms.

The fact that a pre-experiment has been run with great success for some 10 years at the Canada Revenue Agency, and that ways were found there to overcome resistance and blockages, should be grounds enough to argue that the time has come to extend the experiment to a representative group of departments and agencies, so as to be able to determine whether these innovations can be safely generalized to the whole of the Canadian federal public service, and whether there should be exceptions to this regime – where and why.

Kick starting the innovation process

The process could be kick-started by building on the suggestions made by James Lahey that six departments/agencies would be logical candidates for experimenting in this direction: Canada Border Services Agency; Service Canada; Correctional Service of Canada; Statistics Canada; Foreign Affairs, Trade and Development Canada; and Public Works and Government Services (Lahey 2007).

This group of units in the federal public household represents a reasonable variety of organizations in terms of size, types of activities, mixes of policy and operations; and variegated sorts of constraints that would provide a meaningful experiment. The results would help design a workable strategy of extension of the proposed two-punch reform (board of management + competencies approach) to the rest of the federal public household (or at least to a major segment of it).

Conclusion

It has become clear that there is a management vacuum in the Canadian public service governance regime. Observers from all perspectives appear to agree with this diagnosis. Yet very little of substance has been put forward as precise and implementable reforms that might contribute significantly to repairing this flaw.

We have put forward two innovations that might do the job.

We have explained what these innovations entail, and how they would work, and we have conjectured that they would appear to promise much in terms of performance improvement, if the lessons of the CRA experiment are a reasonable basis to build on.

We have underlined a number of blockages that might stand in the way of such innovations, identified the sort of mental prisons and corporatist interests that underpin such blockages, and have argued that there is no reason to believe that such obstacles could not be overcome.

The arrival of a new Clerk of Privy Council on the scene is creating a window of opportunity for public service renewal. Many suggestions will be made to Janice Charette in her first months in office. This paper constitutes our offerings.

References

Aucoin, Peter. 1995. "Canadian Public Management Reform: A Comparative Westminster Perspective," (mimeo).

Aucoin, Peter. 1996. *The New Public Management: Canadian Comparative Perspective*. Montreal, QC: Institute for Research on Public Policy.

Aucoin, Peter. 2007. "Management Boards for Government Departments: Addressing the Governance of Management Vacuum," (unpublished manuscript, July).

Aucoin, Peter. 2012. "New Political Governance in Westminster Systems: Impartial Public Administration and Management

Performance at Risk," *Governance: An international journal of policy, administration and institutions*, 25(2): 177-199.

Canada. 1995. *Framework for Alternative Program Delivery*. Ottawa, ON: Treasury Board Secretariat.

Canada Revenue Agency (CRA). 2011. "Canada Revenue Agency: Creating a Performance-Oriented Culture," Ottawa, ON: Canada Revenue Agency, June.

Canada Revenue Agency (CRA). 2012. "Competency Catalogue: Revised November 2012," Ottawa, ON: Canada Revenue Agency, www.cra.arc.gc.ca/crrs/wrkng/ssssmnt/cmptncy/menue-eng.html [Accessed August 6, 2014].

Canada Revenue Agency (CRA). 2012-13. "Canada Revenue Agency: departmental performance report 2012-13," Ottawa, ON: Canada Revenue Agency, www.cra-arc.gc.ca/gncy/prfrmnc_rprts/2012-2013/vrvw-eng.html [Accessed August 7, 2014].

Canada Revenue Agency (CRA). 2013-14. "Summary of the Board of Management Oversight Framework: Assessment of performance 2013-2014," www.cra-arc.gc.ca/gncy/bomof-cscd/2014-2015/BoMOF-Summary-eng.pdf [Accessed August 7, 2014].

Heintzman, Ralph and Luc Juillet. 2012. "Searching for New Instruments of Accountability: New Political Governance and the Dialectics of Democratic Acountability" in H. Bakvis and M.D. Jarvis (eds.). *From New Public Management to New Political Governance*. Montreal, QC and Kingston, ON: McGill-Queen's University Press, p. 342-379.

Hubbard, Ruth and Gilles Paquet. 2010. *The Black Hole of Public Administration*. Ottawa, ON: University of Ottawa Press.

Hubbard, Ruth and Gilles Paquet. 2014a. *Probing the Bureaucratic Mind: About Canadian Federal Executives*. Ottawa, ON: Invenire Books.

Hubbard, Ruth and Gilles Paquet. 2014b. "Competencies: Part of the Governance Vacuum," *www.optimumonline.ca*, 44(3): 58-73.

Jaques, Elliott. 2002. *The Life and Behavior of Living Organisms.* Westport, CT: Praeger.

Kernaghan, Kenneth. 2007. *A Special Calling: Values, Ethics, and Professional Public Service.* Ottawa, ON: Canada Public Service Agency.

Lahey, James. 2007. "Separate employers and compensation management" in *Expenditure Review of Federal Public Sector: Volume 1 – The Analytical Report and Recommendations* (archived). Ottawa, ON: Treasury Board Secretariat, www.tbs-sct. gc.ca/report/orp/2007/er-ed/vol1/vol113-eng.asp [Accessed November 6, 2014].

McLaughlin, David. 2014. "Five ways to renew the public service," *The Globe and Mail*, August 22, A11.

Office of the Auditor General (OAG). 2008. "Use of New Human Resources Authorities – Canada Revenue Agency" in the *December Report of the Auditor General of Canada,* chapter 6, www. oag-bvg.gc.ca/internet/English/parl_oag_200812_06_e_31830. html [Accessed August 24, 2014].

Paquet, Gilles. 1997. "Alternative Program Delivery: Transforming the Practices of Governance" in R. Ford and D. Zussman (eds.). *Alternative Service Delivery: Sharing Governance in Canada.* Toronto, ON: IPAC/KPMG, p. 31-58 (Reprinted in R. Hubbard and G. Paquet. 2010. *The Black Hole of Public Administration.* Ottawa, ON: University of Ottawa Press, p. 307-330).

Paquet, Gilles. 2014. *Unusual Suspects: Essays on Social Learning Disabilities.* Ottawa, ON: Invenire Books.

Schick, Allen. 2002. "Agencies in Search of Principles," *OECD Journal of Budgeting*, 2(1): 7-26.

Taleb, Nassim N. 2012. *Antifragile – Things that gain from disorder.* New York, NY: Random House.

CONCLUSION

| The Case for Irreverence and Experimentation

"Bad breath isn't near as bad as no breath at all."
William Saroyan

Administrative conservatorship rationalizes and theorizes the role of bureaucrats as guardians of institutional integrity. This is meant to be a counterforce to the supposedly whimsical will of elected officials, in the name of elusive imperatives that only these conservators are supposed to be able to comprehend and defend. This is certainly a stance that greatly legitimizes and empowers bureaucrats when they can claim to be mandated to conserve and preserve the country's mission and values – whatever these words may connote for them. But there is a dark side to this empowerment of the bureaucrats. It fuels conservatorship, risk aversion, deterrence of innovation, slower social learning, and consequently lesser antifragility for our organizations and institutions in our turbulent world.

Appeals to exploratory forays, boldness, risk-taking and innovativeness are unlikely, by themselves, to generate the requisite antidote for these negative side effects. Such sermons are unlikely to have much impact unless ways are found:

1. to shake up the prevailing mindset and dramatically reducing learning disabilities; and

2. to enable the frustrated parties to engage readily in tractable ways to experiment with prototypes likely to provide alternatives to existing flawed arrangements, and to collaborate in order to enhance the antifragility of the social order.

In order to counter the conservatorship tendency to preserve existing arrangements (whether they are satisfactory or not), the attitudes of deference and reverence toward the arrangements inherited from the past have to be expurgated. Irreverence that allows one to probe the limits and the failures of existing arrangements is a fundamental condition if improvements are to be made. Chantal Delsol (2002) ascribes the long period of Europe's dominance in earlier centuries to a fundamental sense of irreverence: an urge to know and to challenge the clerics of all sorts who defend unquestionable absolutes, a drive to learn that sideswiped the taste for security, a rebellious sentiment against all that is obscurantist and claims not to be questionable.

The search for antifragility is based on constant questioning of current practices, on the revisiting of decisions and collective interactions, perspectives, interests, oppositions, and on experimentalism as a method of exploration to learn about new and better ways to coordinate ongoing interactions across various social domains (Paquet 2009).

In this conclusion, we reflect for a moment on the notion of eunomics – "the science, theory or study of good order and workable social arrangements" (Winston 2001), and on the mode of inquiry likely to generate the exploration with new prototypes. We, then, probe very briefly some ways to rekindle our sense of irreverence, and to get to unlearn the reverence reflex that cripples our critical view of the existing arrangements. Finally, we briefly scope the way ahead if we are to reacquire the taste for exploration and experimentation that has been the source of the progressivity and antifragility of the social order in better times, and to feed the redesign process that is called for if we are to acquire a capacity to transform eunomically.

Eunomics

Eunomics is not a well-developed discipline. This is ascribable to the fact that eunomics is a discipline not unlike architecture and design: it purports "to chart its course by a compass that lacks a pole toward which it can point" (*Ibid.*: 62). In the absence of such an absolute, and in the presence of a variety of ends considered desirable by diverse groups of stakeholders, objectives are the result of a compounding blend of diverging views that evolves during the process of elaboration of the ultimate architecture or design outcome.

Given the broad spectrum of views of the diverse stakeholders, coordinating organizations and institutions can only be the result of a process of probing, approximating and accommodating, trying to reconcile non-negotiable external constraints and more or less negotiable differences in perspectives. This process of convergence has been examined carefully by a variety of experts: some scoping the nature of such work in general (Perlmutter 1965); others broadly sketching a practical and workable approach to social learning (Friedmann and Abonyi 1976); still others looking into the minutiae of the work of eunomizing in the light of the work of the likes of architect Frank Gehry (Boland and Collopy 2004); and others have tried to provisionally synthesize all this into a tractable strategy to deal with wicked problems (Paquet 2013: chapter 3).

All these initiatives have helped to clarify the nature of the work called for by the eunomic challenges, but the task remains a work in progress. We only report very quickly here on the general approach of Friedmann and Abonyi that provides a general overview of the social learning process that underpins the production of improved social orders.

They have stylized a simple *social learning exploratory model of policy research* based on four questions about any possible action plan: is it technically feasible; is it socially acceptable; is it too politically destabilizing; is it implementable? In order to respond to these questions, it is necessary to have some appreciation (1) of appropriate theories of reality, (2) of the ways social values are expressed, (3) of the political game within which the design exercise is carried out, and (4) of the ways in which collective action is carried out in the context of interest.

These four pillars of social learning are interconnected, and any change in one affects the others. This paradigm of social practice in policy research is synthesized in Figure 6.

Block B is the locus of the nexus of the different value systems that provide normative guidance, either in the transformation of reality or in the selection of strategies for action. Theory of reality [block A] refers to a symbolic representation and explanation of the complex environment; political strategy [block C] connotes the political game which generates the course of action chosen; collective action [block D] deals with implementation and the interaction with partner groups. Together, these four components come to life in concrete situations.

Conventional approaches to policy research focus on attempts to falsify hypotheses about some objective reality. This is too narrow a focus for policy research when the ground is in motion, and when it is not entirely clear what objectives are sought. For the *social practitioner*, what is central is an effort to create a wholly new, unprecedented situation that, in its possibility for generating new knowledge, goes substantially beyond the initial hypothesis.

The social learning paradigm is built on reflection-in-action, dialogue, and mutual learning by experts and clients: i.e., on an interactive or trans-active style of planning.

The paradigm makes the important epistemological assumption that action hypotheses are verified as 'correct' knowledge only in the course of a social practice that includes the four components of theory [of reality], the configuration of values, strategy, and action. A further epistemological commitment is to the creation of a new reality, and hence to a new knowledge, rather than in establishing the truth-value of propositions in abstraction from the social context to which they are applied (Friedmann and Abonyi 1976: 938).

Similar general ideas have been explored over time by many others, including Carl Taylor (1997).

FIGURE 6: A Social Learning Model of Policy Research

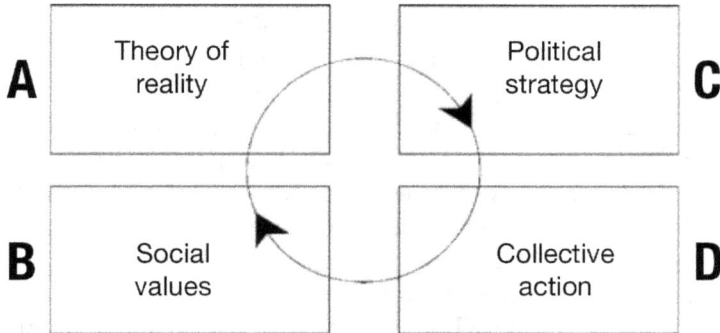

Source: Friedman and Abonyi, 1976, p. 88.

This social learning framework has been used most effectively in analyzing complex phenomena and wicked problems like energy or multiculturalism (Paquet 1989a, b; 2008). But this formulation of the social learning approach has not been sufficiently well operationalized to foster wide adoption and extensive application of this approach to the large number of wicked problems in need of such an approach. What has been missing is a more carefully spelled out version of this approach in stages – not in order that it be applied mechanically and thoughtlessly, but in order to make it more readily useable as a reference protocol for analysts interested in applying it to various issue domains. A sketch of such a reference protocol was proposed in Paquet's *Tackling Wicked Policy Problems* (2013: chapter 3).

Irreverence and prototyping

Irreverence is the courage of insolence, of contrarianism, of the willingness to defend irregular or unusual or atypical approaches. This entails both (1) the capacity to escape from traditional mental prisons, and (2) the capacity to do some innovative thinking outside the box.

The first capacity is acquired through reflexivity, some capacity for critical examination of the assumptions one is expected to make in the discourses in good currency. Often these assumptions are so deeply rooted in the culture that one is not even aware that one is making them. As a result, there is often much resistance to new forms of organizations simply because they are unusual, even though the organizations in place are known to be rather ineffective. Reverence for things, organizations, institutions, or concepts past is bowing uncritically to them. Irreverence is the natural consequence of critical thinking – a willingness to impose a good analysis of the limits of all the arrangements that have come to crystallize in our social order. Crippling epistemologies are perspectives that purport to immunize certain families of arrangements from scrutiny in the name of higher principles. They result in unduly protecting toxic arrangements. Critical thinking demands that all arrangement be subject to scrutiny, and that their eunomic desirability or lack of it be gauged.

Critical thinking is a *manière de voir*, a commitment to not put up with bullshit (Frankfurt 1988, 2005), an engagement to ask why and how always and systematically, and a commitment to insist on maintaining persistent relentless vigilance continually and in all circumstances. This requires from practitioners a *modicum of irreverence* (in order to be able to escape from the mental prisons in good currency, or disciplinary codes, or loosely theorized dogmas).

This vigilant propensity to enhance the *integrity of the process of inquiry* itself requires *thinking skills, a skeptic's worldview,* and *intellectual due process* in a manner that is as free of failures and slippages as possible. However, this is too general a way of stating what has to be done. A more specific way to proceed is to recognize that the flaws at the source of poor critical thinking might be regarded as resulting from three major blockages: *poor critical description* of the context and the organization; *mental prisons* preventing as extensive an examination of the issues as is possible and desirable; and poor appreciation of the *socio-ethical constraints in good currency* within which the inquiry in a particular social system must be conducted (Paquet 2014: chapter 1).

The second capacity entails a willingness and a capacity to think outside the box, and a *certain amount of audacity and courage* to engage in more risky ventures – *la marine en long*, exploring the high seas in search of new continents, and not only the secure *marine en large* that is satisfied to engage in the intellectual equivalent of routine ferry-boating between Cumberland (Ontario) and Gatineau (Quebec) on the Ottawa river.

James March has made five suggestions as a small beginning in this task:

- *treat goals as hypotheses*;
- *treat intuition as real* (i.e., take seriously anything that seems to be outside the present scheme for justifying behaviour);
- *treat hypocrisy as a transition* (i.e., do not treat inconsistency as a vice, and do not allow it to prevent experimentation);
- *treat memory as an enemy* (i.e., consider the possibility that memory prevents experimentation that may well pay off); and,
- *treat experience as a theory* (i.e., allowing experience to have a conceptual status and to drive our thinking just as much as frozen conclusions from the past).

As March would put it, all these procedures represent "a way in which we temporarily suspend the operation of the system of reasoned intelligence. They are playful." (March 1988: 263).

But irreverence by itself is not sufficient.

The new mindset puts a premium on *the highest and best use of imagination, experimentation, and serious play* in the exploration of promising avenues, and the design of viable responses to difficult situations. In that sense, it puts at the core of its inquiries an explicit social learning machine (Paquet 2009: Introduction). The issue must not only be properly contextualized, but must also be subjected to a probing that attempts to make explicit the partiality of the frames used by the different stakeholders in order to generate the requisite blending and blurring of frames that allows fruitful multilogues. There is, therefore, a certain process of reconstruction that accompanies this work: not only searching for responses to the original questions, but wondering whether the original questions were the most useful ones, and exploring ways in which such questions might be modified, transformed, and/or reframed.

This is where the process of experimentation, prototyping, and serious play becomes centrally important. It is not sufficient to ensure open access to tinkering for as many stakeholders as possible; one must also ensure that the appropriate motivations are nurtured, so that all citizens are willing and able to engage in "serious play" (i.e., become truly producers of governance through tinkering with the governance apparatus). Governance relies not only on a much more flexible toolbox, but requires that any formal or binding arrangement be revisited, played with, and adjusted to take into account the evolving diversity of circumstances.

Prototyping means (1) identifying some top requirements as quickly as possible, (2) putting in place a quick-and-dirty provisional medium of co-development, (3) allowing as many interested parties as possible to get involved as partners in designing a better arrangement, (4) encouraging iterative prototyping, and (5) thereby encouraging all, through playing with prototypes, to get a better understanding of the problems, of their priorities, and of themselves (Schrage 2000: 199ff).

Progressivity and antifragility

But this new mindset is not likely to work unless one develops *ab ovo* a more encompassing outlook on the socio-economic scene in order to enrich the appreciation system, and in so doing, make it likely that one will be able to improve the social learning process, the stewarding process, and the wayfinding process, and to lengthen the time horizon. This is what was suggested in the conclusion of Paquet's *Unusual Suspects* (2014).

This need for novel, more open, and more encompassing perspectives must act as a forceful motivation to develop *cranes* (to use the language of Richard Normann 2001: Part V) which send down a hook to lift the observer into a position where new realms are visible that could not be imagined from the ground, allowing a broader and richer perspective.

These cranes should (1) *broaden* our perspective to take into account interactions (social domain), mind frames (cognitive domain), and ecological and power interfaces; (2) *lengthen* our time horizon to take into account a more extended future and the possibility of learning our way out of predicaments; and (3) *elevate* our perspective point to take into account the common public culture within which meso-organizations are nested, and even what is beyond the contingent aspects of the lives of partners in organizations – the transcendent.

There is no standard blueprint for crane construction, but some principles have been proposed by Normann to meet the challenge of designing useful cranes. The crane must be capable of:

- taking stock of the context and of the mega-community;
- upframing, i.e., redefining the out-boundaries of the system one is in;
- moving boldly into future scenarios;
- aiding in wind-tunneling any prototypes that may emerge; and,
- signaling the sort of improved competences, collaboration, and organizational design improvements required.

Two important guideposts emerge from the richer and broader perspectives from the cranes: a focus on progressivity and antifragility. These guideposts shift the attention toward a more dynamic perspective, toward second-order objectives:

- progressivity is not focusing on the achievement of a certain level of desirable outcomes, but on the greatest possible capacity to transform in the direction of more eunomic forms of organization;
- antifragility is not simple resilience (i.e., a capacity to recover after a shock) but a capacity to become ever stronger and more innovative after each new shock.

This sort of perspective is likely to ensure a stewardship that does not aim at satisficing alone, but at generating organizations and institutions that are constantly trying to go beyond the limits (more progressive and more antifragile) as a result of social learning.

Conclusion

There is no guarantee that irregular governance will always generate those results. But there is a possibility it might. This is the philosophy guiding the sort of governance first proposed by Albert Hirschman (1971) – *possibilism* – a deliberate investment (1) in the discovery of paths, however narrow, looking to an outcome that appears to be foreclosed on the basis of probabilistic reasoning alone; and (2) in an approach built on the possibility of increasing the number of ways in which the occurrence of change can be visualized. Such an approach holds the promise of weakening cognitive dissonance and of pointing to presumed obstacles to progress as offering the possibility of being turned into an asset and a spur, a blessing in disguise (Paquet 1993)

All this *may* suffice to counter the toxic effects of conservatorship.

The bold experimentation we urge does not entail any form of rejection of the accomplishments of yesteryear, or denial or amnesia about the social learning of the past, but connotes only a determination to escape from two significant mental prisons – an undue reverence for past arrangements that would immunize them from constant and vigilant critical re-examination, and an undue myopic and uncritical focalization on short-term client-centred efficiencies.

These have driven executives in all sectors (and probably most disastrously federal public sector organizations in Canada because of the size of their operations) to shy away from their burden of office, and the effectiveness, inventiveness, and social learning it commands.

References

Boland, Richard J. and Fred Collopy (eds.). 2004. *Managing by Design*. Stanford, CA: Stanford University Press.

Delsol, Chantal. 2002. *L'irrévérence*. Paris, FR: La Table Ronde.

Frankfurt, Harry G. 1988. *The importance of what we care about*. Cambridge, UK: Cambridge University Press.

Frankfurt, Harry G. 2005. *On Bullshit*. Princeton, NJ: Princeton University Press.

Friedmann, John and George Abonyi. 1976. "Social Learning: A Model for Policy Research," *Environment and Planning*, A, 8(8): 927-940.

Hirschman, Albert O. 1971. *A Bias for Hope*. New Haven, CT: Yale University Press.

March, James G. 1988. "The Technology of Foolishness" in J.G. March. *Decisions and Organizations*. Oxford, UK: Basil Blackwell, p. 253-265.

Normann, Richard. 2001. *Reframing Business: When the Map Changes the Landscape*. Chichester, UK: John Wiley & Sons.

Paquet, Gilles. 1989a. "A Social Learning Framework for a Wicked Problem: The Case of Energy," *Energy Studies Review*, 1(1): 55-69.

Paquet, Gilles. 1989b. "Multiculturalism as National Policy," *Journal of Cultural Economics*, 13(1): 17-34.

Paquet, Gilles. 1993. "Sciences transversales et savoirs d'expérience: the art of trespassing," *Revue générale de droit*, 24(2): 269-281.

Paquet, Gilles. 2008. *Deep Cultural Diversity – A Governance Challenge*. Ottawa, ON: University of Ottawa Press.

Paquet, Gilles. 2009. *Crippling Epistemologies and Governance Failures: A Plea for Experimentalism*. Ottawa, ON: University of Ottawa Press.

Paquet, Gilles. 2013. *Tackling Wicked Policy Problems: Equality, Diversity and Sustainability.* Ottawa, ON: Invenire Books.

Paquet, Gilles. 2014. *Unusual Suspects: Essays on Social Learning Disabilities.* Ottawa, ON: Invenire Books.

Perlmutter, Howard V. 1965. *Towards a Theory and Practice of Social Architecture – The Building of Indispensable Institutions.* London, UK: Tavistock Publications.

Schrage, Michael. 2000. *Serious Play: How the World's Best Companies Simulate to Innovate.* Boston, MA: Harvard Business School Press.

Taylor, Carl A. 1997. "The ACIDD Test: a framework for policy planning and decision-making," *Optimum,* 27(4): 53-62.

Winston, Kenneth I. (ed.). 2001. *The Principles of Social Order – Selected Essays of Lon L. Fuller* (Revised edition). Oxford, UK: Hart Publishing.

| Sources

Paquet, Gilles. 2009. "Ombudspersons as producers of governance" is a revised version of a keynote address delivered at the Joint Ombudsman Conference of the Association of Canadian College and University Ombudspersons (ACCUO), the Forum of Canadian Ombudsman (FCO), and the International Ombudsman Association (IOA) held at Fairmont Queen Elizabeth in Montreal in April, 2009. A slightly different version was published in *www.optimumonline.ca*, 39(3): 6-20.

Paquet, Gilles. 2014. "Super-bureaucrats as *enfants du siècle*," *www.optimumonline.ca*, 44(2): 4-14.

Hubbard, Ruth and Gilles Paquet. 2007. "Public-Private Partnership and the 'porcupine' problem" in Doern, G.B. (ed.). *How Ottawa Spends 2007-08, The Harper Conservatives – Climate of Change*. Montreal, QC and Kingston, ON: McGill-Queen's University Press, p. 254-272.

Hubbard, Ruth and Gilles Paquet. 2013. "Single-Purpose Entities in the Governance of a Multiplex World," in Doern, G.B. and Chris Stoney (eds.). *How Ottawa Spends 2013-14*. Montreal, QC and Kingston, ON: McGill-Queen's University Press, p. 198-208.

Hubbard, Ruth and Gilles Paquet. 2013. "Innovation as Redesign," *www.optimumonline.ca*, 43(4): 1-13.

Hubbard, Ruth and Gilles Paquet. 2014. "Repairing the governance vacuum at the federal level in Canada," *www. optimumonline.ca*, 44(4): 75-86.

Titles in the Collaborative Decentred
Metagovernance Series

Other titles published by INVENIRE

www.ingramcontent.com/pod-product-compliance
Lightning Source LLC
Chambersburg PA
CBHW062056270326
41931CB00013B/3093